Lipton
RECIPE SOUP MIX

RECIPE SECRETS ®

Mealtime Magic

The **Lipton** Kitchens
® Taste Tested Recipes

Project Director: Mindy Sweetwood,
Senior Home Economist

Project Coordinators: Anna Marie Cesario,
Manager—The Lipton Kitchens
Julie Nolan, Senior Home Economist

Project Administrator: Michelle Febres

Recipe Development: The Lipton Kitchens

Test Kitchen Assistant: Liliana Mendoza

Brand Manager: Maria Feicht

Associate Brand Manager: Caryn Friedman

Published by Meredith Custom Publishing,
1912 Grand Ave., Des Moines, IA 50309-3379.
Manufactured in U.S.A.

Pictured on the front cover: Herbed
Chicken and Potatoes (*page 34*)

Pictured on the back cover: Roasted
Potato & Watercress Salad (*page 66*)

Everyday Main-Dish Favorites

GOLDEN CRUSTED STEAK

Prep Time: 10 minutes   *Cook Time: 45 minutes*

1   envelope Lipton Recipe Secrets Onion Soup Mix
½   cup plain dry bread crumbs
¼   cup margarine or butter, melted
2   tablespoons chopped fresh parsley
2   tablespoons Dijon-style mustard
1   clove garlic, finely chopped or ½ teaspoon
     garlic powder
1   boneless beef top round or sirloin steak
     (about 2 lbs.), 2 inches thick and fat trimmed

Preheat oven to 350º.

In small bowl, combine all ingredients except steak. On broiler pan, arrange steak. Press onion mixture on top and sides of steak. Bake uncovered 45 minutes or until steak is done. Makes about 8 servings.

•Also terrific with Lipton Recipe Secrets Onion-Mushroom Soup Mix.

When serving steak, cut into thin slices by cutting diagonally across the grain of the meat.

GOLDEN CRUSTED STEAK

TAMALE PIE

Prep Time: 5 minutes   *Cook Time: 35 minutes*

- 1 tablespoon olive or vegetable oil
- 1 small onion, chopped
- 1 pound ground beef
- 1 envelope Lipton Recipe Secrets Fiesta Herb
    with Red Pepper Soup Mix
- 1 can (14½ oz.) stewed tomatoes, undrained
- ½ cup water
- 1 can (15 to 19 oz.) red kidney beans, rinsed
    and drained
- 1 package (8½ oz.) corn muffin mix

Preheat oven to 400°. In 12-inch skillet, heat oil over medium heat and cook onion, stirring occasionally, 3 minutes or until tender. Stir in ground beef and cook until browned. Stir in Fiesta Herb with Red Pepper Soup Mix blended with tomatoes and water. Bring to a boil over high heat, stirring with spoon to crush tomatoes. Reduce heat to low; stir in beans. Simmer uncovered, stirring occasionally, 10 minutes. Turn into 2-quart casserole.

Prepare corn muffin mix according to package directions. Spoon evenly over casserole. Bake uncovered 15 minutes or until corn topping is golden and filling is hot. Makes about 6 servings.

- •Also terrific with Lipton Recipe Secrets Onion, Onion-Mushroom, Beefy Onion or Beefy Mushroom Soup Mix.

For extra zip, add 1 can (4 oz.) chopped green chilies, undrained, to skillet with soup mix.

SOUPERIOR MEAT LOAF

Prep Time: 15 minutes   *Cook Time: 1 hour*
Stand Time: 10 minutes

- 1 envelope Lipton Recipe Secrets Onion Soup Mix
- 2 pounds ground beef
- 1½ cups fresh bread crumbs
- 2 eggs
- ¾ cup water
- ⅓ cup ketchup

Preheat oven to 350°. In large bowl, combine all ingredients. In 13 x 9-inch baking or roasting pan, shape into loaf. Bake uncovered 1 hour or until done. Let stand 10 minutes before serving. Makes about 8 servings.

- •Also terrific with Lipton Recipe Secrets Beefy Onion, Onion-Mushroom, Italian Herb with Tomato, Savory Herb with Garlic or Fiesta Herb with Red Pepper Soup Mix.

To make fresh bread crumbs, simply place fresh bread in food processor or blender and process until crumbs are very small.

TAMALE PIE

GOLDEN GRILLED FLANK STEAK

Prep Time: 10 minutes   *Cook Time: 20 minutes*

1   **envelope Lipton Recipe Secrets Onion Soup Mix**
1   **jar (12 oz.) apricot or peach preserves**
½   **cup water**
1   **beef flank steak (about 2 lbs.), cut into thin strips**
2   **medium green, red and/or yellow bell peppers, sliced**
   Hot cooked rice

In small bowl, combine Onion Soup Mix, preserves and water; set aside. On foil-lined grill or in bottom of broiler pan, with rack removed, arrange steak and green peppers; top with soup mixture. Grill or broil, turning steak and vegetables once, until steak is done. Serve over hot rice. Makes about 8 servings.

•Also terrific with Lipton Recipe Secrets Onion-Mushroom, Fiesta Herb with Red Pepper, Beefy Onion or Beefy Mushroom Soup Mix.

For a colorful meal, use a combination of red, yellow and green bell peppers.

HOME-STYLE BEEF BRISKET

Prep Time: 10 minutes   *Cook Time: 3 hours*

1   **envelope Lipton Recipe Secrets Onion Soup Mix**
¾   **cup water**
½   **cup ketchup**
1   **teaspoon garlic powder**
½   **teaspoon ground black pepper**
1   **3-pound boneless brisket of beef**

Preheat oven to 325°.

In 13 x 9-inch baking or roasting pan, add Onion Soup Mix blended with water, ketchup, garlic powder and pepper. Add brisket; turn to coat. Loosely cover with aluminum foil and bake 3 hours or until brisket is tender. If desired, thicken gravy. Makes about 8 servings.

•Also terrific with Lipton Recipe Secrets Onion-Mushroom, Beefy Mushroom, Beefy Onion, Savory Herb with Garlic, Fiesta Herb with Red Pepper or Italian Herb with Tomato Soup Mix.

For a heartier meal, add 1 pound potatoes and ½ pound carrots, all cut into chunks, during last hour of roasting.

OLD-FASHIONED POT ROAST

Prep Time: 5 minutes   *Cook Time: 2 hours 35 minutes*

1   3- to 3½-pound boneless beef pot roast
     (rump, chuck or round)
1   envelope Lipton Recipe Secrets Onion Soup Mix
2¼ cups water

In Dutch oven or 6-quart saucepot, brown roast over medium-high heat. Add Onion Soup Mix blended with water. Bring to a boil over high heat. Reduce heat to low and simmer covered, turning occasionally, 2½ hours or until tender. If desired, thicken gravy. Makes about 6 servings.

•Also terrific with Lipton Recipe Secrets Beefy Onion, Beefy Mushroom, Onion-Mushroom, Italian Herb with Tomato or Fiesta Herb with Red Pepper Soup Mix.

For ONION GRAVY, bring 1 envelope Onion Soup Mix blended with 1½ cups water to a boil. Simmer covered, stirring occasionally, 8 minutes. Stir in 2 tablespoons flour blended with ½ cup water. Bring to a boil. Simmer, stirring constantly, 2 minutes or until thickened. Makes about 1¾ cups gravy.

STUFFED BURGERS

Prep Time: 10 minutes   *Cook Time: 8 minutes*

1   envelope Lipton Recipe Secrets Onion Soup Mix
1½ pounds ground beef
3   ounces mozzarella cheese, cut into 6 cubes

In large bowl, combine Onion Soup Mix and ground beef; shape into 6 (6-inch) patties. Place 1 cheese cube in center of each patty. Bring sides over to cover cheese; shape into burger. Grill or broil until done. Serve, if desired, on sesame rolls. Makes about 6 servings.

•Also terrific with Lipton Recipe Secrets Savory Herb with Garlic, Onion-Mushroom, Beefy Onion, Beefy Mushroom or Italian Herb with Tomato Soup Mix.

Experiment stuffing burgers with other cheeses such as cheddar, Monterey Jack or Swiss.

GARDEN BURGERS

Prep Time: 15 minutes   *Cook Time: 45 minutes*

1½ **pounds ground beef or turkey**
  1 **envelope Lipton Recipe Secrets Onion Soup Mix**
  2 **small carrots, finely shredded**
  1 **small zucchini, shredded**
  1 **egg, slightly beaten**
  ¼ **cup plain dry bread crumbs**

Preheat oven to 375°.

In large bowl, combine all ingredients; shape into
6 patties. In 13 x 9-inch baking pan, arrange patties.

Bake uncovered 45 minutes or until done. Serve, if
desired, on hamburger buns or whole wheat rolls.
Makes about 6 servings.

•Also terrific with Lipton Recipe Secrets Savory Herb
with Garlic, Golden Herb with Lemon or Onion-
Mushroom Soup Mix.

When preparing burgers, be sure not to overmix the meat.
Mix ingredients just until blended to produce a better texture.

LIPTON ONION BURGERS

Prep Time: 5 minutes   *Cook Time: 8 minutes*

  1 **envelope Lipton Recipe Secrets Onion Soup Mix**
  2 **pounds ground beef**
  ½ **cup water**

In large bowl, combine all ingredients; shape into
8 patties. Grill or broil until done. Makes about
8 servings.

•Also terrific with Lipton Recipe Secrets Beefy Onion,
Onion-Mushroom, Italian Herb with Tomato, Savory
Herb with Garlic or Fiesta Herb with Red Pepper
Soup Mix.

Serve burgers on fun buns! Try English muffins, pita bread
or even a bagel.

GARDEN BURGERS

SAUCY MEATBALLS

Prep Time: 15 minutes

Cook Time: 30 minutes

1 **pound ground beef**
1 **egg**
⅓ **cup seasoned dry or fresh bread crumbs**
3 **tablespoons olive or vegetable oil**
1 **medium onion, sliced**
1 **envelope Lipton Recipe Secrets Italian Herb
     with Tomato Soup Mix**
1 **cup water**
1 **tablespoon firmly packed brown sugar**
1 **tablespoon red wine vinegar or white vinegar
     Hot cooked noodles or rice**

In medium bowl, combine ground beef, egg and bread crumbs; shape into 16 (1½-inch) meatballs.

In 12-inch skillet, heat oil over medium-high heat and brown meatballs. Cover and continue cooking, stirring occasionally, 15 minutes or until meatballs are done. Remove meatballs and set aside; reserve drippings.

Add onion to reserved drippings and cook over medium heat, stirring occasionally, 3 minutes. Stir in Italian Herb with Tomato Soup Mix blended with water, sugar and vinegar. Bring to a boil over high heat. Reduce heat to low and return meatballs to skillet; heat through. Serve over hot noodles. Makes about 4 servings.

•Also terrific with Lipton Recipe Secrets Fiesta Herb with Red Pepper, Onion-Mushroom, Beefy Mushroom or Beefy Onion Soup Mix.

Try serving on rolls as a sandwich or with toothpicks as an hors d'oeuvre.

Prep Time: 15 minutes   **Cook Time: 1 hour 40 minutes**

2 tablespoons olive or vegetable oil
1½ pounds boneless beef chuck or round steak,
     cut into 1-inch cubes
1 medium onion, cut into thin wedges*
1 envelope Lipton Recipe Secrets Fiesta Herb
     with Red Pepper Soup Mix
1 can (14½ oz.) stewed tomatoes, undrained
½ cup water
2 medium carrots, cut into 1-inch pieces
1 medium green bell pepper, cut into 1-inch pieces
1 cup frozen whole kernel corn, thawed

In Dutch oven or 6-quart saucepot, heat 1 tablespoon oil over medium-high heat and brown beef in two batches; remove beef and set aside.

In same Dutch oven, heat remaining 1 tablespoon oil over medium heat and cook onion, stirring occasionally, 4 minutes. Stir in Fiesta Herb with Red Pepper Soup Mix blended with tomatoes and water. Stir in carrots and beef. Bring to a boil over high heat, stirring up brown bits from bottom of Dutch oven. Reduce heat to low and simmer covered 1 hour. Stir in green pepper and corn. Continue simmering covered 25 minutes or until beef is tender.
Makes about 4 servings.

•Also terrific with Lipton Recipe Secrets Onion, Onion-Mushroom, Beefy Onion or Beefy Mushroom Soup Mix.

*If using Lipton Recipe Secrets Onion, Onion-Mushroom or Beefy Onion Soup Mix, omit onion.

A Dutch oven, which dates to American colonial days, is a large heavy pot with a tight-fitting lid.

TURKEY SAUSAGE & PEPPERS

Prep Time: 10 minutes   *Cook Time: 31 minutes*

- 3   tablespoons olive or vegetable oil
- 1   pound turkey sausage or Italian sausage links, diagonally sliced into 2-inch pieces
- 3   medium green, red and/or yellow bell peppers, cut into 1-inch chunks
- 1   medium onion, cut into 1-inch chunks
- 1   envelope Lipton Recipe Secrets Italian Herb with Tomato Soup Mix
- 1   cup water
      Kaiser or Italian rolls

In 12-inch skillet, heat 1 tablespoon oil over medium-high heat and brown sausage, turning frequently; drain. Remove sausage and set aside. In same skillet, heat remaining 2 tablespoons oil over medium heat and cook green peppers and onion, stirring frequently, 10 minutes or until tender. Stir in Italian Herb with Tomato Soup Mix blended with water. Bring to a boil over high heat. Reduce heat to low and return sausage to skillet. Simmer uncovered 5 minutes or until sausage is done. Serve on rolls. Makes about 6 servings.

●Also terrific with Lipton Recipe Secrets Fiesta Herb with Red Pepper, Savory Herb with Garlic, Golden Herb with Lemon or Onion-Mushroom Soup Mix.

Italian sausage is made from pork and is generally seasoned with garlic and fennel or anise seed.

ITALIAN TURKEY CUTLETS

Prep Time: 5 minutes   *Cook Time: 20 minutes*

- 3   tablespoons margarine or butter
- 4   turkey cutlets or boneless, skinless chicken breast halves (about 1 lb.)
- 1   package (8 or 10 oz.) mushrooms, sliced
- 5   green onions, cut into 2-inch pieces
- 1   envelope Lipton Recipe Secrets Italian Herb with Tomato Soup Mix
- ½   cup water
- ½   cup orange juice

In 12-inch skillet, melt margarine over medium-high heat and lightly brown turkey. Remove turkey and set aside. In same skillet, cook mushrooms and green onions, stirring occasionally, 5 minutes. Add Italian Herb with Tomato Soup Mix blended with water and orange juice. Bring to a boil over high heat. Reduce heat to low; return turkey to skillet. Simmer uncovered 10 minutes or until turkey is done. Makes about 4 servings.

●Also terrific with Lipton Recipe Secrets Onion-Mushroom Soup Mix.

Be sure to heat the margarine or butter in the skillet prior to adding food to prevent sticking.

TURKEY SAUSAGE & PEPPERS

OPEN-FACED FISH SANDWICHES

Prep Time: 10 minutes

Marinate Time: 1–3 hours
Cook Time: 10 minutes

4 **skinless sole or red snapper fillets (about 1½ lbs.)**
1 **envelope Lipton Recipe Secrets Fiesta Herb**
       with Red Pepper Soup Mix
2 **tablespoons lime juice**
1 **tablespoon olive or vegetable oil**
4 **long diagonal slices Italian or French bread,**
       grilled or toasted
    Romaine or leaf lettuce leaves
2 **roasted red peppers, halved (optional)**
¼ **cup plain lowfat yogurt**

In large, shallow nonaluminum baking dish, arrange
fish. Brush both sides of fish with Fiesta Herb with

Red Pepper Soup Mix blended with lime juice and
oil. Cover and marinate in refrigerator, turning
occasionally, 1 to 3 hours. Remove fish, discarding
marinade. Grill or broil fish until done. To serve,
top each piece of bread with lettuce, roasted peppers
and 1 fish fillet. Drizzle with yogurt and garnish, if
desired, with chopped fresh cilantro. Makes about
4 servings.

•Also terrific with Lipton Recipe Secrets Savory Herb
with Garlic or Golden Herb with Lemon Soup Mix.

*One medium lime will yield approximately 1 to
2 tablespoons fresh lime juice.*

TURKEY WITH BLACK BEAN & CORN SALSA

Prep Time: 10 minutes

Cook Time: 15 minutes

3 **tablespoons olive or vegetable oil**
4 **turkey cutlets or boneless, skinless chicken breast**
       halves (about 1 lb.)
1 **medium red onion, chopped**
1 **medium red bell pepper, chopped**
1 **can (15 to 19 oz.) black beans, rinsed and drained**
1 **cup frozen whole kernel corn, thawed**
1 **envelope Lipton Recipe Secrets Fiesta Herb**
       with Red Pepper Soup Mix
1 **cup water**

In 12-inch skillet, heat 2 tablespoons oil over
medium-high heat and cook turkey until done.
Remove turkey and keep warm. In same skillet, heat

remaining 1 tablespoon oil over medium heat and
cook onion and red pepper, stirring frequently,
5 minutes or until tender. Stir in beans, corn and
Fiesta Herb with Red Pepper Soup Mix blended with
water. Bring to a boil over high heat. Reduce heat to
low; simmer uncovered 5 minutes or until sauce is
thickened. Serve salsa over turkey. Makes about
4 servings.

•Also terrific with Lipton Recipe Secrets Italian Herb
with Tomato, Savory Herb with Garlic, Golden Herb
with Lemon or Onion-Mushroom Soup Mix.

*Salsa is the Mexican word for "sauce." It can be a cooked
or fresh mixture.*

OPEN-FACED FISH SANDWICHES

APPLE CIDER PORK CHOPS

Prep Time: 5 minutes   *Cook Time: 1 hour 10 minutes*

2 **tablespoons olive or vegetable oil**
4 **bone-in or boneless pork chops, 1 inch thick**
1 **envelope Lipton Recipe Secrets Onion Soup Mix**
¾ **cup water**
¼ **cup apple cider vinegar**
¼ **cup firmly packed brown sugar**
2 **sweet apples (such as Golden Delicious), cored and cut into quarters**

Preheat oven to 350°. In 12-inch skillet, heat oil over medium-high heat and brown chops. Remove chops to 13 x 9-inch baking or roasting pan and set aside.

In same skillet, bring Onion Soup Mix blended with water, vinegar and sugar to a boil over high heat; pour over chops. Bake covered 35 minutes. Add apples to pan and continue baking covered an additional 25 minutes or until pork is done. Serve, if desired, over hot cooked rice. Makes about 4 servings.

•Also terrific with Lipton Recipe Secrets Onion-Mushroom Soup Mix.

Measuring brown sugar should be done in a "dry" measuring cup, packing the sugar into the cup until level with the top.

SAVORY SAUCED PORK CHOPS

Prep Time: 10 minutes   *Cook Time: 1 hour 10 minutes*

2 **tablespoons olive or vegetable oil**
4 **bone-in or boneless pork chops, 1 inch thick**
2 **red and/or green bell peppers, sliced**
1 **rib celery, sliced**
1 **envelope Lipton Recipe Secrets Onion Soup Mix**
1 **can (15 oz.) tomato sauce**
¼ **cup water**
   Hot cooked noodles

Preheat oven to 350°. In 12-inch skillet, heat oil over medium-high heat and brown chops. Remove chops

to 13 x 9-inch baking or roasting pan and set aside; reserve drippings. Add red peppers and celery to reserved drippings and cook over medium heat, stirring frequently, 5 minutes or until crisp-tender. Stir in Onion Soup Mix blended with tomato sauce and water. Bring to a boil over high heat; pour over chops. Bake covered 1 hour or until chops are done. Serve over hot noodles. Makes about 4 servings.

•Also terrific with Lipton Recipe Secrets Onion-Mushroom Soup Mix.

For the most tender, juicy pork chops, cook to an internal temperature of 160°.

APPLE CIDER PORK CHOPS

SAVORY PORK TENDERLOIN

Prep Time: 20 minutes

Marinate Time: 1–4 hours
Cook Time: 25 minutes

- 1 **envelope Lipton Recipe Secrets Onion Soup Mix**
- 1 **cup water**
- 1 **clove garlic, finely chopped**
- 1½ **pounds pork tenderloin, cut into ¼-inch slices**
- 2 **tablespoons olive or vegetable oil**
- 2 **medium green and/or red bell peppers, cut into thin strips**
- ½ **cup dry red or Marsala wine**

In large, shallow nonaluminum baking dish or plastic bag, blend Onion Soup Mix, water and garlic. Add pork; toss to coat. Cover, or close bag, and marinate in refrigerator, tossing occasionally, 1 to 4 hours.

Remove pork, reserving marinade. In 12-inch skillet, heat oil over medium-high heat and cook green peppers, stirring occasionally, 8 minutes or until tender. Remove peppers and set aside.

In same skillet, brown pork in two batches. Remove pork and set aside. In same skillet, add wine. Bring to a boil over high heat and continue boiling 2 minutes, stirring brown bits from bottom of skillet. Return peppers and reserved marinade to skillet. Bring to a boil over high heat. Reduce heat to low and stir in pork. Simmer uncovered 5 minutes or until heated through. Makes about 6 servings.

•Also terrific with Lipton Recipe Secrets Italian Herb with Tomato, Fiesta Herb with Red Pepper, Onion-Mushroom, Beefy Onion or Beefy Mushroom Soup Mix.

Use a dry Marsala wine that has a rich, smoky flavor. Sweet Marsala wine is used for desserts.

ONION-CRUSTED PORK CHOPS

Prep Time: 10 minutes   *Cook Time: 30 minutes*

- 1 **envelope Lipton Recipe Secrets Onion Soup Mix**
- ⅓ **cup plain dry bread crumbs**
- 4 **bone-in or boneless pork chops, 1 inch thick**
- 2 **to 4 tablespoons Dijon-style mustard**

Preheat oven to 375°.

In small bowl, combine Onion Soup Mix and bread crumbs. Brush both sides of chops with mustard, then dip in soup mixture until evenly coated. In 13 x 9-inch baking or roasting pan, arrange chops. Bake uncovered, turning once, 30 minutes or until done. Makes about 4 servings.

Variations:

ONION-CRUSTED LAMB CHOPS: Substitute 8 lamb loin or rib chops for pork. Prepare as directed, decreasing bake time to 15 minutes.

ONION-CRUSTED VEAL CHOPS: Substitute 4 veal loin or rib chops for pork. Prepare as directed, decreasing bake time to 25 minutes.

•Also terrific with Lipton Recipe Secrets Onion-Mushroom Soup Mix.

> *Dijon mustard is made from mustard seeds blended with salt, spices and white wine.*

25 NEW WAYS WITH CHICKEN

CHICKEN WITH GREEN BEANS

Prep Time: 15 minutes   *Cook Time: 20 minutes*

1 pound boneless, skinless chicken breasts,
   cut into strips
2 tablespoons Dijon-style mustard
2 tablespoons margarine or butter
½ pound green beans, each cut in half
2 medium carrots, cut into 2-inch-long matchsticks
1 medium onion, sliced
1 envelope Lipton Recipe Secrets Golden Herb
   with Lemon Soup Mix
1 cup water
   Hot cooked rice

Dip chicken in mustard. In 12-inch skillet, melt margarine over medium-high heat and brown chicken. Remove chicken and set aside. In same skillet, cook green beans, carrots and onion over medium heat, stirring occasionally, 5 minutes. Stir in Golden Herb with Lemon Soup Mix blended with water. Bring to a boil over high heat. Reduce heat to low and simmer covered 5 minutes or until green beans are crisp-tender. Return chicken to skillet and simmer covered an additional 3 minutes or until chicken is done. Serve with hot rice. Makes about 4 servings.

• Also terrific with Lipton Recipe Secrets Savory Herb with Garlic or Golden Onion Soup Mix.

Ingredients cut into matchsticks are referred to as "julienne." To julienne carrots, first cut into 2-inch pieces. Thinly slice lengthwise, then stack the slices and cut into thin strips.

CHICKEN WITH GREEN BEANS

Prep Time: 15 minutes　　　　　　　　　　　　　　*Cook Time: 25 minutes*

1　**envelope Lipton Recipe Secrets Italian Herb with Tomato Soup Mix**
½　**cup plain dry bread crumbs**
6　**ounces fontina, Swiss, Jarlsberg, provolone or mozzarella cheese, cut into 6 equal slices**
6　**boneless, skinless chicken breast halves (about 1½ lbs.), pounded ¼ inch thick**
3　**tablespoons margarine or butter, melted**

Preheat oven to 350°.

In medium bowl, combine Italian Herb with Tomato Soup Mix and bread crumbs. Place 1 slice cheese in center of each chicken breast half. Roll chicken around cheese and secure with wooden toothpicks. Dip chicken breasts in margarine, then soup mixture until evenly coated. In 13 x 9-inch baking or roasting pan, arrange chicken; drizzle with remaining margarine. Bake uncovered 25 minutes or until chicken is done. Remove toothpicks before serving. Makes about 6 servings.

This recipe is great for entertaining! Serve with steamed broccoli and carrots.

Variations:

PROSCIUTTO-STUFFED CHICKEN BREASTS: Place 1 slice prosciutto or cooked ham on each chicken breast half. Top with cheese and continue as directed.

SPINACH-STUFFED CHICKEN BREASTS: Evenly divide 1 package (10 oz.) frozen chopped spinach, thawed and drained, on each chicken breast half. Top with cheese and continue as directed.

•Also terrific with Lipton Recipe Secrets Fiesta Herb with Red Pepper, Savory Herb with Garlic or Golden Herb with Lemon Soup Mix.

STUFFED CHICKEN BREASTS

TORTILLA CRUNCH CHICKEN FINGERS

Prep Time: 15 minutes   *Cook Time: 12 minutes*

- 1   envelope Lipton Recipe Secrets Fiesta Herb with Red Pepper Soup Mix
- 1   cup finely crushed plain tortilla chips or corn flakes (about 3 oz.)
- 1½ pounds boneless, skinless chicken breasts, cut into strips
- 1   egg
- 2   tablespoons water
- 2   tablespoons margarine or butter, melted

Preheat oven to 400°.

In medium bowl, combine Fiesta Herb with Red Pepper Soup Mix and tortilla chips. In large plastic bag or bowl, combine chicken and egg beaten with water until evenly coated. Remove chicken and dip in tortilla mixture until evenly coated; discard bag. On 15½ x 10½ x 1-inch jelly-roll pan sprayed with nonstick cooking spray, arrange chicken; drizzle with margarine. Bake uncovered 12 minutes or until chicken is done. Makes about 24 chicken fingers.

• Also terrific with Lipton Recipe Secrets Italian Herb with Tomato or Savory Herb with Garlic Soup Mix.

Serve the chicken fingers with your favorite fresh or prepared salsa.

FIESTA CHICKEN CHILI

Prep Time: 10 minutes   *Cook Time: 45 minutes*

- 2   tablespoons olive or vegetable oil
- 1½ pounds boneless, skinless chicken thighs, cut into 1-inch pieces
- 1   large onion, chopped
- 1   envelope Lipton Recipe Secrets Fiesta Herb with Red Pepper Soup Mix
- 1   can (14½ oz.) whole peeled tomatoes, undrained and coarsely chopped
- 1   can (15 to 19 oz.) black or red kidney beans, undrained
- 1   cup frozen whole kernel corn

In Dutch oven or 6-quart saucepot, heat oil over medium-high heat and brown chicken in two batches. Remove chicken and set aside; reserve drippings. Add onion to reserved drippings and cook over medium heat, stirring occasionally, 5 minutes. Return chicken to Dutch oven. Stir in Fiesta Herb with Red Pepper Soup Mix blended with tomatoes, beans and corn, stirring up brown bits from bottom of Dutch oven. Bring to a boil over high heat. Reduce heat to low and simmer covered, stirring occasionally, 25 minutes or until chicken is done. Makes about 6 servings.

Chili is great served with corn bread or biscuits and a mixed green salad.

TORTILLA CRUNCH CHICKEN FINGERS

LEMON CHICKEN 'N RICE

Prep Time: 10 minutes   *Cook Time: 50 minutes*

1 cup uncooked regular or converted rice
1 medium red bell pepper, sliced
1 medium onion, cut into wedges
1 envelope Lipton Recipe Secrets Golden Herb
    with Lemon Soup Mix
1½ cups water
1 cup orange juice
½ teaspoon salt
4 boneless, skinless chicken breast halves (about 1 lb.)

Preheat oven to 350°.

In 13 x 9-inch casserole, combine uncooked rice, red pepper, onion and Golden Herb with Lemon Soup

Mix blended with water, orange juice and salt. Arrange chicken on rice, spooning some liquid over chicken. Bake covered 40 minutes. Remove cover and bake an additional 10 minutes or until chicken and rice are done. Makes about 4 servings.

•Also terrific with Lipton Recipe Secrets Savory Herb with Garlic or Golden Onion Soup Mix.

Garnish with orange slices and fresh chopped parsley.

ZESTY GLAZED CHICKEN

Prep Time: 5 minutes   *Cook Time: 45 minutes*

1 2½- to 3-pound chicken, cut into serving pieces
    (with or without skin)
1 envelope Lipton Recipe Secrets Fiesta Herb
    with Red Pepper Soup Mix
2 tablespoons water
1 tablespoon firmly packed brown sugar

Preheat oven to 350°.

In 13 x 9-inch baking or roasting pan, arrange chicken. Brush with Fiesta Herb with Red Pepper

Soup Mix blended with water and sugar. Bake uncovered 45 minutes or until chicken is done. Makes about 4 servings.

•Also terrific with Lipton Recipe Secrets Savory Herb with Garlic, Golden Herb with Lemon or Golden Onion Soup Mix.

Use a pastry brush to easily brush soup mixture on chicken.

CHICKEN PAPRIKA

Prep Time: 5 minutes   *Cook Time: 1 hour*

2   tablespoons margarine or butter
1   2½- to 3-pound chicken, cut into serving pieces
      (with or without skin)
1   envelope Lipton Recipe Secrets Onion Soup Mix
1¾ cups water
1   teaspoon paprika
1   tablespoon all-purpose flour
1   container (8 oz.) sour cream
    Hot cooked noodles or rice

In 12-inch skillet, melt margarine over medium-high heat and brown chicken; drain. Stir in Onion Soup Mix blended with 1½ cups water and paprika. Bring to a boil over high heat. Reduce heat to low and simmer covered 45 minutes or until chicken is done. Remove chicken; keep warm.

In same skillet, stir in flour blended with remaining ¼ cup water. Bring to a boil over high heat. Reduce heat to low and simmer uncovered, stirring frequently, 2 minutes or until sauce is thickened. Remove from heat and with wire whisk, blend in sour cream. Serve chicken and sauce over hot noodles. Makes about 4 servings.

•Also terrific with Lipton Recipe Secrets Golden Onion, Savory Herb with Garlic, Golden Herb with Lemon, Italian Herb with Tomato, Fiesta Herb with Red Pepper or Onion-Mushroom Soup Mix.

Paprika is made from grinding several kinds of chili peppers. The types of peppers used determines how hot the paprika is.

GRILLED CHICKEN WITH CITRUS SALSA

Prep Time: 25 minutes

Marinate Time: 3–24 hours
Cook Time: 8 minutes

1 envelope Lipton Recipe Secrets Golden Herb
   with Lemon Soup Mix
¼ cup water
3 tablespoons olive or vegetable oil
4 boneless, skinless chicken breast halves (about 1 lb.)
2 medium oranges
1 medium pink grapefruit*
1 jalapeño pepper, seeded and finely chopped**
¼ cup finely chopped red onion
¼ cup finely chopped red bell pepper
2 teaspoons lime juice
¼ teaspoon salt

In large, shallow nonaluminum baking dish or plastic bag, blend Golden Herb with Lemon Soup Mix, water and oil. Add chicken; turn to coat. Cover, or close bag, and marinate in refrigerator, turning occasionally, 3 to 24 hours.

Meanwhile, for citrus salsa, section oranges and grapefruit over small bowl to catch any juices (see *** at right). Cut orange and grapefruit sections into 1-inch pieces; place in bowl with any juice. Stir in jalapeño pepper, onion, red pepper, lime juice and salt. Cover and refrigerate until serving.

Grill or broil chicken, turning once, 8 minutes or until chicken is done. Slice each chicken breast and arrange, if desired, over salad greens. Top with citrus salsa. Makes about 4 servings.

*If grapefruit is not very sweet, sweeten citrus salsa with sugar, to taste.

**Since jalapeño peppers contain oils that can burn eyes, lips and skin, we recommend wearing plastic gloves when handling them. Also, wash hands thoroughly after handling peppers.

***To section oranges and grapefruit: Using paring knife, peel fruit, removing outer peel and pith (white membrane). Cut along both sides of each dividing membrane and lift out sections from center; discard any seeds.

•Also terrific with Lipton Recipe Secrets Savory Herb with Garlic Soup Mix.

Citrus salsa may be made up to 1 day ahead and stored covered in the refrigerator.

GRILLED CHICKEN WITH CITRUS SALSA

LEMON-TWIST CHICKEN AMANDINE

Prep Time: 5 minutes   *Cook Time: 20 minutes*

⅓ **cup sliced almonds**
2 **tablespoons olive or vegetable oil**
4 **boneless, skinless chicken breast halves (about 1 lb.)**
1 **envelope Lipton Recipe Secrets Golden Herb with Lemon Soup Mix**
1¼ **cups water**
1 **tablespoon honey**
1 **teaspoon soy sauce**
   Hot cooked noodles or rice

In 12-inch skillet, cook almonds over medium heat, stirring frequently, until golden. Remove almonds and set aside. In same skillet, heat oil over medium-high heat and brown chicken. Stir in almonds and Golden Herb with Lemon Soup Mix blended with water, honey and soy sauce. Bring to a boil over high heat. Reduce heat to low and simmer uncovered 10 minutes or until chicken is done. Serve over hot noodles. Makes about 4 servings.

•Also terrific with Lipton Recipe Secrets Savory Herb with Garlic or Golden Onion Soup Mix.

Amandine is French for "garnished with almonds."

CHICKEN WITH A TOUCH OF ORANGE

Prep Time: 10 minutes   *Cook Time: 40 minutes*

3 **tablespoons margarine or butter**
6 **boneless, skinless chicken breast halves (about 1½ lbs.)**
1 **medium bulb fennel, sliced (about 3 cups) or 3 ribs celery, sliced**
1 **large red onion, sliced**
1 **envelope Lipton Recipe Secrets Italian Herb with Tomato Soup Mix**
½ **cup water**
½ **cup orange juice**

In 12-inch skillet, melt margarine over medium-high heat and brown chicken; remove and set aside. In same skillet, cook fennel and onion over medium heat, stirring occasionally, 10 minutes. Add Italian Herb with Tomato Soup Mix blended with water and orange juice. Bring to a boil over high heat. Reduce heat to low; return chicken to skillet. Simmer covered 15 minutes or until chicken is done. Makes about 6 servings.

•Also terrific with Lipton Recipe Secrets Fiesta Herb with Red Pepper, Savory Herb with Garlic or Golden Herb with Lemon Soup Mix.

Fennel has celery-like stems and green feathery tops. Stems may be eaten raw or cooked. Tops may be used as a garnish.

LEMON-TWIST CHICKEN AMANDINE

HERB-BAKED CHICKEN

Prep Time: 10 minutes   *Cook Time: 30 minutes*

1   2½- to 3-pound chicken, cut into serving pieces
1   medium onion, chopped
1   medium zucchini, halved crosswise then
      sliced lengthwise
1   envelope Lipton Recipe Secrets Golden Herb
      with Lemon Soup Mix
1   can (14½ oz.) stewed tomatoes, undrained
      Hot cooked rice or noodles

Preheat oven to 350°. In 13 x 9-inch baking or roasting pan, arrange chicken, onion and zucchini. Pour Golden Herb with Lemon Soup Mix blended with tomatoes over chicken. Bake uncovered, basting occasionally, 30 minutes or until chicken is done. Serve with hot rice. Makes about 4 servings.

•Also terrific with Lipton Recipe Secrets Savory Herb with Garlic Soup Mix.

Complete this meal with a mixed green salad, iced tea and frozen yogurt sundaes.

HONEY DIJON CHICKEN

Prep Time: 10 minutes   *Cook Time: 20 minutes*

¼   cup margarine or butter, melted
2   tablespoons Dijon-style mustard
1   tablespoon honey
6   boneless, skinless chicken breast halves
      (about 1½ lbs.)
1   envelope Lipton Recipe Secrets Savory Herb
      with Garlic Soup Mix
½   cup plain dry bread crumbs

Preheat oven to 375°. In small bowl, combine margarine, mustard and honey. Dip chicken in margarine mixture, then Savory Herb with Garlic Soup Mix combined with bread crumbs until evenly coated. In 13 x 9-inch baking or roasting pan, arrange chicken. Bake uncovered 20 minutes or until chicken is done. Makes about 6 servings.

•Also terrific with Lipton Recipe Secrets Golden Herb with Lemon or Golden Onion Soup Mix.

For HONEY DIJON CHICKEN FINGERS, cut chicken into strips and dip in mustard mixture, then soup mixture. Bake uncovered at 400° on 15½ x 10½ x 1-inch jelly-roll pan sprayed with nonstick cooking spray for 15 minutes or until chicken is done.

ROASTED LEMON-PEPPER CHICKEN

Prep Time: 10 minutes **L** *Cook Time: 45 minutes*

1 **2½- to 3-pound chicken, cut into serving pieces**
1 **envelope Lipton Recipe Secrets Golden Herb with Lemon Soup Mix**
2 **tablespoons water**
1 **tablespoon olive or vegetable oil**
¼ **teaspoon cracked black pepper**

Preheat oven to 375°. In large plastic bag or bowl, add all ingredients. Close bag and shake, or toss in bowl, until chicken is evenly coated. In 13 x 9-inch baking or roasting pan, arrange chicken; discard bag. Bake uncovered 45 minutes or until chicken is done. Makes about 4 servings.

•Also terrific with Lipton Recipe Secrets Savory Herb with Garlic Soup Mix.

Serve with Lipton Rice & Sauce–Chicken & Parmesan Risotto for a complementary side dish.

CREAMY CHICKEN TARRAGON

Prep Time: 5 minutes **L** *Cook Time: 1 hour*

2 **tablespoons olive or vegetable oil**
1 **2½- to 3-pound chicken, cut into serving pieces (with or without skin)**
1 **envelope Lipton Recipe Secrets Onion Soup Mix**
1 **cup water**
½ **cup dry white wine or water**
½ **teaspoon dried tarragon leaves, crushed**
2 **tablespoons all-purpose flour**
½ **cup milk**

In 12-inch skillet, heat oil over medium-high heat and brown chicken; drain. Stir in Onion Soup Mix blended with water, wine and tarragon. Bring to a boil over high heat. Reduce heat to low and simmer covered 45 minutes or until chicken is done. Remove chicken to serving platter; keep warm.

In same skillet, stir in flour blended with milk. Bring just to the boiling point over high heat. Reduce heat to low and simmer uncovered, stirring constantly, 5 minutes or until sauce is thickened. Pour sauce over chicken. Makes about 4 servings.

•Also terrific with Lipton Recipe Secrets Onion-Mushroom or Golden Onion Soup Mix.

Tarragon has a distinctive licorice-like flavor. Crush dried herbs to release more flavor while cooking.

HERBED CHICKEN AND POTATOES

Prep Time: 10 minutes   *Cook Time: 50 minutes*

1   **pound all-purpose potatoes, thinly sliced**
8   **lemon slices* (optional)**
4   **bone-in chicken breast halves (about 2 lbs.)****
1   **envelope Lipton Recipe Secrets Savory Herb
      with Garlic Soup Mix**
⅓   **cup water**
1   **tablespoon olive or vegetable oil**

Preheat oven to 375°.

In 13 x 9-inch baking or roasting pan, combine potatoes and lemon; arrange chicken on top. Pour Savory Herb with Garlic Soup Mix blended with water and oil over chicken and potatoes. Bake uncovered

50 minutes or until chicken is done and potatoes are tender. Makes about 4 servings.

**Variation: Also delicious substituting 1 (2½- to 3-lb.) chicken, cut into serving pieces, for chicken breast halves.

•Also terrific with Lipton Recipe Secrets Golden Herb with Lemon Soup Mix.

*If using Lipton Recipe Secrets Golden Herb with Lemon Soup Mix, omit lemon slices.

All-purpose potatoes can be stored in a cool, dark place for up to 2 weeks.

ROASTED CHICKEN WITH RED ONION

Prep Time: 5 minutes   *Cook Time: 45 minutes*

1   **2½- to 3-pound chicken, cut into serving pieces**
1   **large red onion, cut into rings**
1   **envelope Lipton Recipe Secrets Savory Herb
      with Garlic Soup Mix**
¼   **cup orange juice**

Preheat oven to 375°.

In 13 x 9-inch baking or roasting pan, arrange chicken and onion. Pour Savory Herb with Garlic

Soup Mix blended with orange juice over chicken. Bake uncovered 45 minutes or until chicken is done. Makes about 4 servings.

•Also terrific with Lipton Recipe Secrets Golden Herb with Lemon Soup Mix.

Serve with Lipton Rice & Sauce—Chicken Flavor or Pilaf for a complementary side dish.

HERBED CHICKEN AND POTATOES

CHICKEN WITH SAVORY TOMATO SAUCE

Prep Time: 5 minutes   *Cook Time: 25 minutes*

1   tablespoon olive or vegetable oil
4   boneless, skinless chicken breast halves (about 1 lb.)
1   envelope Lipton Recipe Secrets Savory Herb
      with Garlic Soup Mix
1   can (15 oz.) tomato sauce
¼   cup dry white wine or water
¼   cup whipping or heavy cream
⅛   teaspoon crushed red pepper flakes (optional)
      Hot cooked noodles

In 12-inch skillet, heat oil over medium-high heat and
brown chicken. Stir in Savory Herb with Garlic Soup

Mix blended with tomato sauce, wine, cream and
red pepper flakes. Bring to the boiling point over
high heat. Reduce heat to low and simmer covered,
turning chicken once, 20 minutes or until chicken is
done and sauce is slightly thickened. Serve over hot
noodles. Makes about 4 servings.

*For a change of pace, try serving chicken over white,
brown or wild rice.*

CRUNCHY NUTTY CHICKEN

Prep Time: 10 minutes   *Cook Time: 20 minutes*

4   boneless, skinless chicken breast halves (about 1 lb.)
¼   cup margarine or butter, melted
1   envelope Lipton Recipe Secrets Savory Herb
      with Garlic Soup Mix
¼   cup plain dry bread crumbs
⅓   cup finely chopped almonds

Preheat oven to 375°.

Dip chicken in margarine, then Savory Herb with
Garlic Soup Mix combined with bread crumbs and

almonds until evenly coated. In 13 x 9-inch baking
or roasting pan, arrange chicken. Bake uncovered
20 minutes or until chicken is done. Makes about
4 servings.

•Also terrific with Lipton Recipe Secrets Golden
Herb with Lemon, Italian Herb with Tomato, Fiesta
Herb with Red Pepper or Golden Onion Soup Mix.

*Serve with Lipton Noodles & Sauce—Butter
for a complementary side dish.*

APRICOT-GLAZED CHICKEN BREASTS

Prep Time: 10 minutes

Cook Time: 20 minutes

- 1 envelope Lipton Recipe Secrets Savory Herb
  with Garlic Soup Mix
- ½ cup apricot preserves
- 1 tablespoon soy sauce
- 6 boneless, skinless chicken breast halves
  (about 1½ lbs.)
- 2 medium zucchini, sliced
- 1 medium red or green bell pepper, sliced
  Hot cooked rice

In small bowl, thoroughly combine Savory Herb
with Garlic Soup Mix, preserves and soy sauce;
set aside. In bottom of broiler pan, with rack
removed, arrange chicken breasts, zucchini and red
pepper; top with soup mixture. Broil, turning once,
10 minutes or until chicken is done. Serve over hot
rice. Makes about 6 servings.

•Also terrific with Lipton Recipe Secrets Golden Herb
with Lemon or Golden Onion Soup Mix.

*For a different flavor, try substituting peach preserves
for apricot preserves.*

SAVORY LEMON CHICKEN

Prep Time: 10 minutes

Marinate Time: 30 minutes–3 hours
Cook Time: 8 minutes

- 1 envelope Lipton Recipe Secrets Golden Herb
  with Lemon Soup Mix
- ½ cup sour cream
- 1 tablespoon Dijon-style mustard
- ¼ teaspoon ground ginger (optional)
- 4 boneless, skinless chicken breast halves (about 1 lb.)

In large, shallow nonaluminum baking dish or
plastic bag, blend all ingredients except chicken.
Add chicken; turn to coat. Cover, or close bag, and
marinate in refrigerator, turning once, 30 minutes
to 3 hours.

Remove chicken, reserving marinade. On broiler pan
sprayed with nonstick cooking spray, arrange chicken
and top with marinade mixture. Broil or grill, turning
once, until chicken is done. Makes about 4 servings.

•Also terrific with Lipton Recipe Secrets Savory Herb
with Garlic or Golden Onion Soup Mix.

*For a restaurant-style chicken salad, simply slice chicken
and serve over mixed greens.*

SAVORY CHICKEN 'N MUSHROOMS

Prep Time: 10 minutes   - L -   *Cook Time: 1 hour*

- 4 **slices bacon, chopped**
- 1 **2½- to 3-pound chicken, cut into serving pieces**
     (with or without skin)
- 1 **package (8 or 10 oz.) mushrooms, quartered**
- 1 **clove garlic, finely chopped**
- 1 **envelope Lipton Recipe Secrets Onion Soup Mix**
- 1¼ **cups water**
- ½ **cup dry red wine or water**
- ½ **teaspoon dried oregano or thyme leaves, crushed**

In Dutch oven or 6-quart saucepot, cook bacon over medium-high heat 3 minutes or until crisp. Remove bacon and set aside; reserve drippings. Add chicken to reserved drippings and brown over medium-high heat. Remove chicken and set aside; reserve drippings. Add mushrooms and garlic to reserved drippings and cook over medium heat, stirring frequently, 4 minutes. Return chicken and bacon to Dutch oven. Stir in Onion Soup Mix blended with water, wine and oregano. Bring to a boil over high heat. Reduce heat to low and simmer covered 40 minutes or until chicken is done. Serve, if desired, with creamy mashed potatoes. Makes about 4 servings.

Substitute 1½ teaspoons chopped fresh herbs for the dried. Add during the last 5 minutes of cooking.

CLASSIC HERBED CHICKEN

Prep Time: 10 minutes   - L -   *Cook Time: 25 minutes*

- 1 **envelope Lipton Recipe Secrets Savory Herb**
     with Garlic Soup Mix
- ⅓ **cup mayonnaise**
- 2 **tablespoons water**
- 4 **boneless, skinless chicken breast halves (about 1 lb.)**

Preheat oven to 425°.

In small bowl, blend Savory Herb with Garlic Soup Mix, mayonnaise and water. In 13 x 9-inch baking or roasting pan sprayed with nonstick cooking spray, arrange chicken; brush with ½ of the soup mixture. Bake uncovered, turning once and brushing with remaining soup mixture, 25 minutes or until chicken is done. Makes about 4 servings.

•Also terrific with Lipton Recipe Secrets Golden Herb with Lemon or Fiesta Herb with Red Pepper Soup Mix.

Serve with Lipton Pasta & Sauce—Chicken Primavera for a complementary side dish.

SAVORY CHICKEN 'N MUSHROOMS

CHICKEN CASSOULET

Prep Time: 10 minutes ·L· *Cook Time: 20 minutes*

- **2 tablespoons olive or vegetable oil**
- **4 boneless, skinless chicken breast halves (about 1 lb.)**
- **2 medium carrots, sliced**
- **½ cup sliced onion**
- **1 can (19 oz.) cannellini or white kidney beans, rinsed and drained**
- **1 envelope Lipton Recipe Secrets Golden Herb with Lemon Soup Mix**
- **1 cup water**

In 12-inch skillet, heat oil over medium-high heat and brown chicken. Remove chicken and set aside; reserve drippings. Add carrots and onion to reserved drippings and cook over medium heat, stirring occasionally, 5 minutes. Stir in beans and Golden Herb with Lemon Soup Mix blended with water. Return chicken to skillet. Reduce heat to low and simmer covered 10 minutes or until chicken is done. Makes about 4 servings.

•Also terrific with Lipton Recipe Secrets Savory Herb with Garlic, Fiesta Herb with Red Pepper or Italian Herb with Tomato Soup Mix.

Cassoulet is a classic French dish featuring white beans and assorted meats or poultry. It is simmered to blend the flavors.

CHICKEN TUSCANY

Prep Time: 10 minutes ·L· *Cook Time: 1 hour*

- **1 tablespoon olive or vegetable oil**
- **1 2½- to 3-pound chicken, cut into serving pieces (with or without skin)**
- **1 medium green bell pepper, cut into strips or 2 ribs celery, cut into ½-inch slices**
- **1¾ cups sliced mushrooms (about 4 oz.)**
- **1 envelope Lipton Recipe Secrets Onion Soup Mix**
- **½ cup orange juice**
- **1 can (14½ oz.) whole peeled tomatoes, undrained and chopped**
- **2 tablespoons firmly packed brown sugar**
- **½ cup pitted ripe olives, sliced (optional)**

In 12-inch skillet, heat oil over medium-high heat and brown chicken. Remove chicken and set aside; reserve drippings. Add green pepper and mushrooms to reserved drippings and cook over medium heat, stirring occasionally, 2 minutes. Return chicken to skillet. Stir in Onion Soup Mix blended with orange juice, tomatoes and sugar. Bring to a boil over high heat. Reduce heat to low and simmer covered 45 minutes or until chicken is done. Stir in olives. Serve, if desired, with hot cooked pasta or rice. Makes about 4 servings.

Tuscany is a region in Northern Italy that centers around Florence.

SANTA FE CHICKEN

Prep Time: 15 minutes

Marinate Time: 30 minutes
Cook Time: 15 minutes

1   envelope Lipton Recipe Secrets Onion Soup Mix
¼   cup olive or vegetable oil
¼   cup water
1   tablespoon lime juice
1   pound boneless, skinless chicken breasts,
     cut into strips
1   medium red, green and/or yellow bell pepper,
     cut into strips
1   medium onion, cut into wedges
     Flour tortillas, warmed (optional)
     Tortilla Topper* (optional)

In large, shallow nonaluminum baking dish or plastic bag, blend Onion Soup Mix, oil, water and lime juice. Add chicken, red pepper and onion; toss to coat. Cover, or close bag, and marinate in refrigerator, tossing once, 30 minutes.

Preheat oven to 450°. In 13 x 9-inch baking or roasting pan or nonaluminum baking dish, arrange chicken, vegetables and marinade mixture; discard bag. Bake uncovered 15 minutes or until chicken is done and vegetables are tender. Serve with tortillas and Tortilla Topper. Makes about 4 servings.

*Tortilla Topper: In small bowl, combine ½ cup sour cream or plain yogurt, 1 tablespoon chopped fresh cilantro and 1 teaspoon lime juice.

•Also terrific with Lipton Recipe Secrets Golden Herb with Lemon, Fiesta Herb with Red Pepper or Savory Herb with Garlic Soup Mix.

Tortillas are generally available in the refrigerated section in your supermarket.

MEATLESS
MAIN
DISHES

GRILLED VEGETABLE SANDWICHES

Prep Time: 10 minutes   *Cook Time: 10 minutes*

2   **pounds assorted fresh vegetables***
1   **envelope Lipton Recipe Secrets Onion Soup Mix**
⅓   **cup olive or vegetable oil**
2   **tablespoons balsamic vinegar or red wine vinegar**
½   **teaspoon dried basil leaves, crushed**
4   **(8-inch) pita breads, warmed**
4   **ounces crumbled Montrachet or shredded**
     mozzarella cheese

In large bowl, combine vegetables. Stir in Onion Soup Mix blended with oil, vinegar and basil, tossing until evenly coated. Grill or broil vegetables until tender. To serve, cut 1-inch strip off each pita. Fill with vegetables and sprinkle with cheese. Garnish, if desired, with shredded lettuce and sliced tomato. Makes about 4 servings.

*Use any of the following, sliced: red, green or yellow bell peppers, mushrooms, zucchini or eggplant.

•Also terrific with Lipton Recipe Secrets Savory Herb with Garlic, Golden Herb with Lemon, Italian Herb with Tomato, Fiesta Herb with Red Pepper or Golden Onion Soup Mix.

If the rack on your grill is too wide for sliced vegetables, try using a grill screen. They're available in the housewares section of department stores or hardware stores.

GRILLED VEGETABLE SANDWICHES

CHEESY EGGPLANT CASSEROLE

Prep Time: 15 minutes   *Cook Time: 31 minutes*

- 1   **envelope Lipton Recipe Secrets Italian Herb with Tomato Soup Mix**
- ½   **cup plain dry bread crumbs**
- 1   **medium eggplant, peeled and cut into ¼-inch-thick slices**
- 1   **egg**
- 2   **tablespoons water**
- 4   **tablespoons olive or vegetable oil**
- 2   **cups shredded mozzarella cheese (about 8 oz.)**
- 1   **tablespoon grated Parmesan cheese**

Preheat oven to 350°. In bowl, combine Italian Herb with Tomato Soup Mix with bread crumbs. Dip eggplant in egg beaten with water, then crumb mixture until evenly coated. In 12-inch skillet, heat 2 tablespoons oil and cook ½ of the eggplant over medium heat, turning once, 3 minutes or until golden. Repeat with remaining oil and eggplant, using additional oil if needed. In 11 x 7-inch baking dish, layer ½ of the eggplant, then 1 cup mozzarella cheese; repeat. Sprinkle with Parmesan cheese. Bake covered 25 minutes or until heated through. Makes about 4 servings.

•Also terrific with Lipton Recipe Secrets Savory Herb with Garlic or Fiesta Herb with Red Pepper Soup Mix.

To peel eggplant, cut it crosswise in half and place flat side down on cutting board. Cut skin away while turning eggplant.

ROASTED VEGETABLE PIZZA

Prep Time: 10 minutes   *Cook Time: 30 minutes*

- 1   **envelope Lipton Recipe Secrets Onion Soup Mix**
- 1½ **pounds assorted fresh vegetables***
- 2   **tablespoons olive or vegetable oil**
- 1   **12-inch Italian bread or pizza shell (about 16 oz.)**
- 1   **cup shredded Monterey Jack or mozzarella cheese (about 4 oz.)**

Preheat oven to 450°. In large plastic bag or bowl, add Onion Soup Mix, vegetables and oil. Close bag and shake, or toss in bowl, until vegetables are evenly coated. In 13 x 9-inch baking or roasting pan, arrange vegetables; discard bag. Bake uncovered, stirring once, 20 minutes or until vegetables are tender. On baking sheet, arrange pizza shell; top with vegetables, then cheese. Bake uncovered 10 minutes or until cheese is melted. Makes about 4 servings.

*Use any of the following, sliced: red, green or yellow bell peppers, red onion, zucchini, plum tomatoes or mushrooms.

•Also terrific with Lipton Recipe Secrets Fiesta Herb with Red Pepper, Savory Herb with Garlic, Golden Herb with Lemon or Italian Herb with Tomato Soup Mix.

Vegetables may be roasted ahead of time for easy planning and a super-quick meal.

FRESH VEGETABLES OVER COUSCOUS

Prep Time: 10 minutes

Cook Time: 8 minutes

3   tablespoons olive or vegetable oil
2   pounds assorted fresh vegetables*
1   can (15 to 19 oz.) chick peas or garbanzos, rinsed
     and drained
¼   cup golden raisins (optional)
1   envelope Lipton Recipe Secrets Savory Herb
     with Garlic Soup Mix
1½ cups water
2   tablespoons lemon juice**
½   teaspoon ground cumin (optional)
1   box (10 oz.) couscous, prepared according to
     package directions

In 12-inch skillet, heat oil over medium heat and cook vegetables, stirring occasionally, 5 minutes or until tender. Add chick peas, raisins and Savory Herb with Garlic Soup Mix blended with water, lemon juice and cumin. Cook, stirring occasionally, 3 minutes. Serve over hot couscous. Makes about 4 servings.

*Use any combination of the following, sliced: zucchini, yellow squash, red onions, carrots, mushrooms or red or green bell peppers.

•Also terrific with Lipton Recipe Secrets Golden Herb with Lemon, Fiesta Herb with Red Pepper or Italian Herb with Tomato Soup Mix.

**If using Lipton Recipe Secrets Golden Herb with Lemon Soup Mix, omit lemon juice.

Fresh vegetable mixture may also be served over hot cooked white, brown or wild rice.

ZESTY BARLEY STEW

Prep Time: 10 minutes   *Cook Time: 26 minutes*

2 tablespoons olive or vegetable oil
3 medium carrots, sliced
3 ribs celery, sliced
1 medium onion, chopped
½ cup quick-cooking barley
1 envelope Lipton Recipe Secrets Fiesta Herb with Red Pepper Soup Mix
4 cups water
½ teaspoon salt
1 can (17 oz.) whole kernel corn, drained
1 can (15 to 19 oz.) red kidney beans, rinsed and drained

In Dutch oven or 6-quart saucepot, heat oil over medium heat and cook carrots, celery and onion, stirring occasionally, 10 minutes or until tender. Stir in barley and Fiesta Herb with Red Pepper Soup Mix blended with water and salt. Bring to a boil over high heat. Reduce heat to low and simmer covered, 10 minutes. Stir in corn and beans; cook an additional 5 minutes or until barley is tender. Makes about 6 servings.

•Also terrific with Lipton Recipe Secrets Savory Herb with Garlic, Italian Herb with Tomato or Golden Onion Soup Mix.

Quick-cooking barley is a time-saver since it cooks in 10 minutes. Regular barley takes 45 to 50 minutes!

HEARTY LENTIL STEW

Prep Time: 10 minutes   *Cook Time: 40 minutes*

2 tablespoons olive or vegetable oil
3 medium carrots, sliced
3 ribs celery, sliced
1 cup lentils
3 cups water
1 envelope Lipton Recipe Secrets Fiesta Herb with Red Pepper Soup Mix
1 tablespoon cider vinegar or red wine vinegar
Hot cooked brown rice, couscous or pasta

In 3-quart saucepan, heat oil over medium heat and cook carrots and celery, stirring occasionally, 3 minutes. Add lentils and cook 1 minute. Stir in

2 cups water. Bring to a boil over high heat. Reduce heat to low and simmer covered, stirring occasionally, 25 minutes. Stir in Fiesta Herb with Red Pepper Soup Mix blended with remaining 1 cup water. Simmer covered an additional 10 minutes or until lentils are tender. Stir in vinegar. Serve over hot rice. Makes about 4 servings.

•Also terrific with Lipton Recipe Secrets Savory Herb with Garlic, Onion-Mushroom, Onion or Italian Herb with Tomato Soup Mix.

Before cooking, lentils should be inspected for stones or foreign objects, then rinsed in water.

MEATLESS MAIN DISHES

ZESTY BARLEY STEW

PINWHEEL CHEESE QUICHE

Prep Time: 20 minutes   *Cook Time: 30 minutes*

2   **tablespoons margarine or butter**
2   **cups sliced mushrooms**
6   **green onions, sliced (about 2 cups)**
1   **package (8 oz.) refrigerated crescent rolls,
      separated into 8 triangles**
1   **envelope Lipton Recipe Secrets Golden Herb
      with Lemon Soup Mix**
½   **cup half and half**
4   **eggs, beaten**
1   **cup shredded Monterey Jack
      or mozzarella cheese (about 4 oz.)**

Preheat oven to 375°. In 12-inch skillet, melt margarine over medium heat and cook mushrooms and green onions, stirring, 5 minutes or until tender.

Remove from heat and set aside. In 9-inch pie plate sprayed with nonstick cooking spray, arrange crescent roll triangles in a spoke pattern with narrow tips hanging over rim of pie plate about 2 inches. Press dough onto bottom and up sides of pie plate forming a full crust. In medium bowl, combine Golden Herb with Lemon Soup Mix blended with half and half and eggs. Stir in cheese and mushroom mixture. Pour into prepared crust. Bring tips of dough over filling towards center. Bake uncovered 30 minutes or until knife inserted in center comes out clean. Makes about 6 servings.

•Also terrific with Lipton Recipe Secrets Savory Herb with Garlic Soup Mix.

Serve for breakfast or brunch, or serve with soup and salad for a hearty lunch or dinner.

FIESTA-STYLE POLENTA

Prep Time: 10 minutes   *Cook Time: 20 minutes*

1   **envelope Lipton Recipe Secrets Fiesta Herb
      with Red Pepper Soup Mix**
4   **cups water**
¾   **cup yellow cornmeal**
2   **cups shredded Monterey Jack, mozzarella or
      cheddar cheese (about 8 oz.)**
1   **pound of your favorite vegetables, grilled
      or sautéed (about 4 cups)**

In 3-quart saucepan, bring Fiesta Herb with Red Pepper Soup Mix blended with water to a boil over

high heat. Reduce heat to medium and with wire whisk, stirring constantly, gradually and very slowly blend in cornmeal. Reduce heat to low and simmer uncovered, whisking frequently, 15 minutes or until mixture is very thick. Stir in cheese until melted. To serve, spoon polenta on serving platter and top with hot vegetables. Makes about 4 servings.

•Also terrific with Lipton Recipe Secrets Italian Herb with Tomato, Golden Herb with Lemon or Golden Onion Soup Mix.

Polenta may also be poured into a pan, cooled and cut into squares. The squares may be eaten at room temperature or sautéed in a skillet and served hot.

PINWHEEL CHEESE QUICHE

FIESTA BURRITO BAKE

Prep Time: 15 minutes　　　　　　　　　　　　　　*Cook Time: 25 minutes*

1　envelope Lipton Recipe Secrets Fiesta Herb
　　with Red Pepper Soup Mix
1　can (15 oz.) refried beans
½　cup sour cream
¼　cup water
10　(6-inch) flour tortillas
1　medium tomato, coarsely chopped
1　cup shredded cheddar cheese (about 4 oz.)

Preheat oven to 375°. In small bowl, combine Fiesta Herb with Red Pepper Soup Mix, beans, sour cream and water. Evenly spoon bean mixture onto tortillas, then roll. In 13 x 9-inch baking dish sprayed with nonstick cooking spray, arrange rolled tortillas; top with tomato, then cheese. Bake covered 15 minutes. Remove cover and continue baking 10 minutes or until cheese is melted and tortillas are heated through. Serve, if desired, with shredded lettuce, sour cream and guacamole. Makes 10 tortillas.

•Also terrific with Lipton Recipe Secrets Italian Herb with Tomato Soup Mix.

For BURRITO DIP, in shallow 1-quart casserole, combine all ingredients except tortillas. Bake at 350° for 15 minutes or until heated through. Serve with tortilla chips.

ASPARAGUS CHEESE TART

Prep Time: 10 minutes　　　　　　　　　　　　　　*Cook Time: 50 minutes*
　　　　　　　　　　　　　　　　　　　　　　　　　　Stand Time: 10 minutes

1　9-inch unbaked pastry shell
3　eggs
½　pint (8 oz.) light cream or half and half
1　envelope Lipton Recipe Secrets Savory Herb
　　with Garlic Soup Mix
4　to 8 ounces goat cheese, crumbled
8　ounces asparagus or zucchini, cut into ½-inch pieces
　　and steamed

Preheat oven to 375°. Bake pastry shell 10 minutes. Remove from oven and let stand on wire rack.

In large bowl, beat eggs, cream and Savory Herb with Garlic Soup Mix. Stir in cheese and asparagus. Pour into pastry shell. Bake uncovered 40 minutes or until knife inserted in center comes out clean. Let stand 10 minutes before serving. Makes about 6 servings.

•Also terrific with Lipton Recipe Secrets Fiesta Herb with Red Pepper, Italian Herb with Tomato or Golden Onion Soup Mix.

Goat cheese, also called "chèvre," which is French for "goat," is a pure white cheese made from goat's milk.

FIESTA BURRITO BAKE

CHEESE & VEGETABLE STRATA

Prep Time: 15 minutes

Cook Time: 31 minutes
Stand Time: 10 minutes

- 4   tablespoons margarine or butter
- 2   cups sliced mushrooms
- 1   small zucchini, halved lengthwise and sliced
- ½   cup chopped onion
- ½   cup chopped red bell pepper
- 8   slices lightly toasted white or whole wheat bread
      or 4 English muffins, halved and toasted lightly
- 1   envelope Lipton Recipe Secrets Golden Herb
      with Lemon Soup Mix
- 2   cups milk
- 3   eggs, beaten
- 2   cups shredded cheddar or mozzarella cheese
      (about 8 oz.)

Preheat oven to 400°.

In 12-inch skillet, melt 2 tablespoons margarine over medium heat and cook mushrooms, zucchini, onion and red pepper, stirring occasionally, 6 minutes or until tender. Remove from heat and set aside.

Evenly spread remaining 2 tablespoons margarine over bread. Cut each bread slice into quarters or each English muffin half into halves. In 12 x 8-inch baking dish sprayed with nonstick cooking spray, arrange bread, slightly overlapping slices.

In large bowl, blend Golden Herb with Lemon Soup Mix, milk and eggs. Add vegetable mixture and 1½ cups cheese. Pour over bread in baking dish. Sprinkle with remaining ½ cup cheese. Bake uncovered 25 minutes or until knife inserted in center comes out clean. Let stand 10 minutes before serving. Makes about 6 servings.

•Also terrific with Lipton Recipe Secrets Savory Herb with Garlic or Golden Onion Soup Mix.

"Strata" means layers and in this recipe refers to the layering of bread, vegetables and cheese.

SPINACH SOUFFLÉ

Prep Time: 10 minutes   *Cook Time: 25 minutes*

4 tablespoons grated Parmesan cheese
3 tablespoons margarine or butter
1 tablespoon all-purpose flour
1 envelope Lipton Recipe Secrets Onion Soup Mix
1¼ cups milk
4 eggs, separated
4 ounces Jarlsberg or Swiss cheese, shredded
1 package (10 oz.) frozen chopped spinach, thawed and squeezed dry
¼ teaspoon dried tarragon leaves, crushed (optional)

Preheat oven to 375°.

Spray 2-quart soufflé dish or round casserole with nonstick cooking spray and sprinkle evenly with 1 tablespoon Parmesan cheese; set aside.

In 3-quart saucepan, melt margarine over medium-high heat and cook flour, stirring occasionally, 1 minute. Stir in Onion Soup Mix blended with milk. Cook, stirring constantly, 2 minutes or until thickened. In small bowl, beat egg yolks until smooth. Using wire whisk, gradually blend ½ cup hot milk mixture into yolks, then blend back into milk mixture. Let mixture cool slightly. Stir in Jarlsberg cheese, spinach, tarragon and remaining 3 tablespoons Parmesan cheese.

In large bowl, beat egg whites until stiff peaks form. Fold beaten egg whites into spinach mixture. Pour into prepared dish and bake uncovered 20 minutes or until lightly browned and puffed. Makes about 4 servings.

•Also terrific with Lipton Recipe Secrets Savory Herb with Garlic, Golden Herb with Lemon, Fiesta Herb with Red Pepper, Golden Onion or Italian Herb with Tomato Soup Mix.

A classic soufflé dish can be purchased in specialty kitchenware shops or in the housewares section of department stores.

PASTA PIZAZZ

RAVIOLI STEW

Prep Time: 10 minutes   *Cook Time: 12 minutes*

2 tablespoons olive or vegetable oil
1 medium onion, chopped
2 medium carrots, diced
2 ribs celery, diced
1 medium green bell pepper, chopped
1 clove garlic, finely chopped*
1 can (15 to 19 oz.) red kidney beans, rinsed
    and drained
4 plum tomatoes, chopped
1 envelope Lipton Recipe Secrets Golden Herb
    with Lemon Soup Mix
2½ cups water
1 package (8 or 10 oz.) refrigerated cheese ravioli

In Dutch oven or 6-quart saucepot, heat oil over medium heat and cook onion, carrots, celery, green pepper and garlic, stirring, 5 minutes or until tender. Stir in beans, tomatoes and Golden Herb with Lemon Soup Mix blended with water. Bring to a boil over high heat. Stir in ravioli. Reduce heat to medium; cook, stirring gently, 5 minutes or until ravioli are tender. Serve with grated Parmesan cheese. Makes about 4 (2-cup) servings.

•Also terrific with Lipton Recipe Secrets Savory Herb with Garlic Soup Mix.

*If using Lipton Recipe Secrets Savory Herb with Garlic Soup Mix, omit garlic.

Fresh pasta, as in the refrigerated ravioli, contains lots of moisture, therefore, it requires a very short cook time.

RAVIOLI STEW

GRILLED CHICKEN & PASTA

Prep Time: 10 minutes

Cook Time: 15 minutes

1   **envelope Lipton Recipe Secrets Golden Herb with Lemon Soup Mix**
½   **cup water**
1   **pound boneless, skinless chicken breasts**
8   **ounces bow tie or rotelle pasta**
8   **ounces broccoli florets and/or sliced carrots**
½   **cup sour cream**
1   **medium tomato, seeded and chopped**

In small bowl, blend Golden Herb with Lemon Soup Mix and water; reserve ½ of the mixture. Pour remaining mixture on chicken; grill or broil chicken until done. Cut chicken into strips; set aside. Meanwhile, cook pasta according to package directions, adding broccoli during last 4 minutes of cooking; drain. In large bowl, blend reserved soup mixture with sour cream. Stir in pasta, chicken and tomato until evenly coated. Season, if desired, with salt and ground black pepper. Makes about 4 servings.

•Also terrific with Lipton Recipe Secrets Savory Herb with Garlic or Golden Onion Soup Mix.

To seed a tomato, cut in half horizontally. Gently squeeze out the juice and seeds, shaking, if necessary, to remove all seeds.

PASTA WITH FRESH TOMATO SAUCE

Prep Time: 10 minutes

Stand Time: 30 minutes
Cook Time: 10 minutes

2   **large tomatoes, diced**
1   **large yellow and/or red bell pepper, finely chopped**
½   **cup finely chopped red onion**
1   **envelope Lipton Recipe Secrets Savory Herb with Garlic Soup Mix**
2   **tablespoons olive or vegetable oil**
1   **tablespoon balsamic vinegar or red wine vinegar**
8   **ounces rotelle or bow tie pasta**

In large nonaluminum bowl, combine tomatoes, yellow pepper and red onion. Stir in Savory Herb with Garlic Soup Mix blended with oil and vinegar. Cover and let stand at room temperature to let flavors blend, about 30 minutes. Meanwhile, cook pasta according to package directions; drain. Toss tomato mixture with hot pasta. Serve immediately or refrigerate and serve cold. Makes about 2 main-dish or 4 side-dish servings.

•Also terrific with Lipton Recipe Secrets Golden Herb with Lemon Soup Mix.

For BRUSCHETTA, spoon this fresh tomato mixture on toasted Italian or French bread slices.

GRILLED CHICKEN & PASTA

SAVORY LO MEIN

2 tablespoons olive or vegetable oil
1 medium clove garlic, finely chopped*
1 small head bok choy, cut into 2-inch pieces
    (about 5 cups)**
1 envelope Lipton Recipe Secrets Onion Soup Mix
1 cup water
2 tablespoons sherry (optional)
1 teaspoon soy sauce
¼ teaspoon ground ginger (optional)
8 ounces linguine or spaghetti, cooked and drained

In 12-inch skillet, heat oil over medium heat and cook garlic and bok choy, stirring frequently, 10 minutes or until crisp-tender. Stir in Onion Soup Mix blended with water, sherry, soy sauce and ginger. Bring to a boil over high heat. Reduce heat to low and simmer uncovered, stirring occasionally, 5 minutes. Toss with hot linguine. Makes about 4 servings.

**Substitution: Use 5 cups coarsely shredded green cabbage. Decrease 10-minute cook time to 3 minutes.

•Also terrific with Lipton Recipe Secrets Onion-Mushroom, Savory Herb with Garlic, Golden Herb with Lemon or Golden Onion Soup Mix.

*If using Lipton Recipe Secrets Savory Herb with Garlic Soup Mix, omit garlic.

Bok choy, also known as Chinese white cabbage, has long white stalks and dark green leaves. Use it raw or cooked.

FIESTA MAC 'N CHEESE

1 pound ground beef
1 envelope Lipton Recipe Secrets Fiesta Herb
    with Red Pepper Soup Mix
1 cup water
12 ounces American or pasteurized process cheese,
    cut into cubes
8 ounces elbow macaroni, cooked and drained

In 12-inch skillet, brown ground beef over medium-high heat; drain. Stir in Fiesta Herb with Red Pepper Soup Mix blended with water and cook 3 minutes. Stir in cheese until melted. Toss with hot macaroni. Serve immediately. Makes about 4 servings.

•Also terrific with Lipton Recipe Secrets Savory Herb with Garlic or Italian Herb with Tomato Soup Mix.

Ground chuck will provide the best flavor. Ground round contains less fat, and ground sirloin is the most lean.

VEGETABLE PASTA PIZZA

Prep Time: 15 minutes　　　　　　　　　　　　　*Cook Time: 40 minutes*

8　ounces angel hair pasta, cooked and drained
½　cup grated Parmesan cheese
3　tablespoons margarine or butter, melted
2　tablespoons olive or vegetable oil
1　medium onion, sliced
1　medium red bell pepper, cut into strips
1　envelope Lipton Recipe Secrets Savory Herb
　　with Garlic Soup Mix
1½　cups milk
1　package (10 oz.) frozen chopped spinach,
　　thawed and squeezed dry
4　eggs, slightly beaten
1　cup shredded mozzarella cheese (about 4 oz.)

Preheat oven to 350°. In medium bowl, combine
cooked pasta, ¼ cup Parmesan cheese and margarine.

In 12-inch pizza or 15½ x 10½ x 1-inch jelly-roll pan,
spread pasta mixture evenly over bottom. Bake
uncovered 15 minutes. Meanwhile, in 10-inch skillet,
heat oil over medium heat and cook onion, stirring
occasionally, 2 minutes. Add red pepper and cook
2 minutes. Add Savory Herb with Garlic Soup Mix
blended with milk. Bring to the boiling point over
high heat. Remove from heat and stir in spinach, eggs
and remaining ¼ cup Parmesan cheese. Spread over
pasta crust; sprinkle with mozzarella cheese. Bake an
additional 25 minutes or until filling is set. Makes
about 4 servings.

•Also terrific with Lipton Recipe Secrets Golden Herb
with Lemon, Italian Herb with Tomato or Fiesta Herb
with Red Pepper Soup Mix.

*Also called capellini, angel hair pasta is the thinnest
spaghetti-like pasta.*

CHEESY FETTUCCINE

Prep Time: 5 minutes　　　　　　　　　　　　　*Cook Time: 20 minutes*

¼　cup margarine or butter
1　envelope Lipton Recipe Secrets Onion Soup Mix
1　pint (16 oz.) whipping or heavy cream or light cream
1　package (16 oz.) fettuccine or medium egg noodles,
　　cooked and drained
1　cup shredded Swiss or mozzarella cheese
　　(about 4 oz.)
½　cup grated Parmesan cheese

In 2-quart saucepan, melt margarine over medium
heat and stir in Onion Soup Mix blended with cream;
heat through, but do not boil. Toss with hot
fettuccine and cheeses. Serve immediately. Makes
about 4 main-dish or 8 side-dish servings.

•Also terrific with Lipton Recipe Secrets Onion-
Mushroom Soup Mix.

*Try CHEESY FETTUCCINE PRIMAVERA by adding
cooked fresh, frozen or canned vegetables to hot fettuccine.*

PASTA FRITTATA

Prep Time: 15 minutes   *Cook Time: 10 minutes*

6 eggs
¼ cup milk
1 envelope Lipton Recipe Secrets Onion Soup Mix
¼ cup grated Parmesan cheese
1 tablespoon PLUS 1 teaspoon olive or vegetable oil
1 small zucchini, diced
2 plum tomatoes, diced
1 cup elbow macaroni, cooked and drained
2 tablespoons plain dry bread crumbs
1 tablespoon chopped fresh basil or ½ teaspoon dried
   basil leaves, crushed
   Prepared marinara sauce, heated (optional)

In medium bowl, beat eggs, milk, Onion Soup Mix and cheese; set aside. In 10-inch nonstick skillet, heat 1 tablespoon oil over medium heat and cook zucchini, stirring, 2 minutes or until tender. Stir in tomatoes and macaroni. Stir in egg mixture; cook uncovered over low heat (do not stir) 5 minutes or until eggs are almost set. Meanwhile, in small bowl, combine bread crumbs, basil and remaining 1 teaspoon oil; sprinkle over egg mixture. Continue cooking 2 minutes or until eggs are set. To serve, cut into wedges. Serve with warm marinara sauce. Makes about 4 servings.

•Also terrific with Lipton Recipe Secrets Savory Herb with Garlic, Golden Herb with Lemon, Onion-Mushroom or Golden Onion Soup Mix.

A frittata is an Italian omelet cooked over low heat and served open-faced, not flipped in half as in a French omelet.

QUICK SKILLET DINNER

Prep Time: 5 minutes   *Cook Time: 22 minutes*

1 pound ground beef
1 envelope Lipton Recipe Secrets Onion Soup Mix
1 can (14 to 16 oz.) whole peeled tomatoes, undrained
1 container (8 oz.) sour cream
8 ounces fusilli, medium shells or penne pasta,
   cooked and drained

In 12-inch skillet, brown ground beef over medium-high heat; drain. Stir in Onion Soup Mix blended with tomatoes. Bring to a boil over high heat, stirring with spoon to crush tomatoes. Reduce heat to low and simmer uncovered, stirring, 15 minutes. Remove from heat and with wire whisk, blend in sour cream, then toss with hot pasta. Makes about 4 servings.

•Also terrific with Lipton Recipe Secrets Savory Herb with Garlic, Beefy Onion or Onion-Mushroom Soup Mix.

Pasta contains complex carbohydrates that take time to digest, leaving you feeling full for a longer period of time.

PASTA FRITTATA

ROASTED VEGETABLES WITH FETTUCCINE

Prep Time: 15 minutes

Cook Time: 20 minutes

2 pounds assorted fresh vegetables*
1 envelope Lipton Recipe Secrets Golden Herb
      with Lemon Soup Mix
3 tablespoons olive or vegetable oil
½ cup light cream, whipping or heavy cream
      or half and half
¼ cup grated Parmesan cheese
8 ounces fettuccine or linguine, cooked and drained

Preheat oven to 450°.

In large plastic bag or bowl, combine vegetables,
Golden Herb with Lemon Soup Mix and oil. Close
bag and shake, or toss in bowl, until vegetables are
evenly coated. In 13 x 9-inch baking or roasting pan,
arrange vegetables; discard bag.

Bake uncovered, stirring once, 20 minutes or until
vegetables are tender. Stir in light cream and cheese
until evenly coated. Toss with hot fettuccine. Serve,
if desired, with additional grated Parmesan cheese
and freshly ground black pepper. Makes about
2 main-dish or 4 side-dish servings.

*Use any of the following, cut into 1-inch chunks:
red, green or yellow bell peppers, zucchini, yellow
squash, red onion or eggplant.

•Also terrific with Lipton Recipe Secrets Savory Herb
with Garlic, Fiesta Herb with Red Pepper, Golden
Onion or Italian Herb with Tomato Soup Mix.

*Try serving with spinach fettuccine or with "straw and hay"—
a combination of regular egg and spinach fettuccine.*

ROASTED VEGETABLES WITH FETTUCCINE

FETTUCCINE IN CREAMY GARLIC SAUCE

Prep Time: 10 minutes   *Cook Time: 10 minutes*

    2 tablespoons margarine or butter
    1 medium onion, thinly sliced
    1 cup frozen green peas, thawed
    4 ounces prosciutto or cooked ham, cut into strips
    1 envelope Lipton Recipe Secrets Savory Herb
         with Garlic Soup Mix
 1½ cups water
    ½ cup whipping or heavy cream or light cream
    8 ounces fettuccine or linguine, cooked and drained

In 10-inch skillet, melt margarine over medium heat and cook onion, stirring occasionally, 3 minutes or until tender. Add peas, prosciutto and Savory Herb with Garlic Soup Mix blended with water and cream. Bring to the boiling point over high heat. Reduce heat to low and simmer, stirring occasionally, 2 minutes. Toss with hot fettuccine. Makes about 2 main-dish or 4 side-dish servings.

•Also terrific with Lipton Recipe Secrets Golden Herb with Lemon, Fiesta Herb with Red Pepper or Italian Herb with Tomato Soup Mix.

Frozen peas may be thawed in the microwave at HIGH (Full Power) 3 minutes, stirring occasionally.

MEDITERRANEAN PASTA

Prep Time: 10 minutes   *Cook Time: 15 minutes*

    ¼ cup olive or vegetable oil
    1 large eggplant (about 1 lb.), peeled
         and cut into 1-inch cubes
    1 large onion, chopped
    1 envelope Lipton Recipe Secrets Italian Herb
         with Tomato Soup Mix
 1¼ cups water
    ½ cup pitted ripe olives, sliced
    8 ounces medium shells or penne pasta, cooked
         and drained
    4 ounces feta cheese, crumbled (optional)

In 12-inch skillet, heat oil over medium heat and cook eggplant and onion, covered, stirring occasionally, 10 minutes or until tender. Add Italian Herb with Tomato Soup Mix blended with water. Bring to boil over high heat; continue boiling 2 minutes. Stir in olives. Toss with hot pasta, then sprinkle with cheese. Makes about 2 main-dish or 4 side-dish servings.

•Also terrific with Lipton Recipe Secrets Fiesta Herb with Red Pepper, Golden Herb with Lemon or Savory Herb with Garlic Soup Mix.

Feta cheese is a Greek cheese made from sheep's, goat's or cow's milk.

PENNE PASTA WITH VEGETABLES

Prep Time: 15 minutes   *Cook Time: 10 minutes*

- 2 tablespoons olive or vegetable oil
- ½ pound asparagus or zucchini, thinly sliced
- ¼ pound crimini or white mushrooms, quartered
- 1 large clove garlic, finely chopped*
- 1 can (14 oz.) artichoke hearts, drained, rinsed and chopped
- 1 envelope Lipton Recipe Secrets Fiesta Herb with Red Pepper Soup Mix
- 1½ cups water
- 8 ounces penne or ziti pasta, cooked and drained
- 1 tablespoon chopped pitted ripe olives (optional)

In 12-inch skillet, heat oil over medium heat and cook asparagus, mushrooms and garlic, stirring occasionally, 5 minutes. Stir in artichoke hearts and Fiesta Herb with Red Pepper Soup Mix blended with water. Cook, stirring occasionally, 2 minutes or until mixture thickens. Toss with hot pasta. Sprinkle with olives and garnish, if desired, with Parmesan cheese curls. Makes about 2 main-dish or 4 side-dish servings.

•Also terrific with Lipton Recipe Secrets Italian Herb with Tomato, Savory Herb with Garlic or Golden Herb with Lemon Soup Mix.

*If using Lipton Recipe Secrets Savory Herb with Garlic Soup Mix, omit garlic.

Crimini mushrooms are firm, brown and meaty, and are related to the common white mushroom.

MUSHROOM-LACED FETTUCCINE

Prep Time: 10 minutes   *Cook Time: 10 minutes*

- 3 tablespoons margarine or butter
- ½ pound portabella, crimini, shiitake, white, morels and/or porcini mushrooms, sliced
- 1 envelope Lipton Recipe Secrets Savory Herb with Garlic Soup Mix
- 1¼ cups milk
- 8 ounces fettuccine or linguine, cooked and drained

In 10-inch skillet, melt margarine over medium heat and cook mushrooms, stirring occasionally, 6 minutes or until tender. Add Savory Herb with Garlic Soup Mix blended with milk. Bring to the boiling point over high heat, stirring frequently. Toss with hot fettuccine. Serve immediately. Makes about 2 main-dish or 4 side-dish servings.

•Also terrific with Lipton Recipe Secrets Golden Herb with Lemon, Golden Onion or Fiesta Herb with Red Pepper Soup Mix.

Store fresh mushrooms in a paper bag in the refrigerator. Here's an easy slicing tip: Use an egg slicer!

SPECTACULAR SIDE DISHES

ROASTED POTATO & WATERCRESS SALAD

Prep Time: 10 minutes   **Cook Time: 40 minutes**

1   envelope Lipton Recipe Secrets Savory Herb
    with Garlic Soup Mix
⅓   cup PLUS 2 tablespoons olive or vegetable oil
2   pounds small red potatoes, cut into quarters
2   tablespoons white wine vinegar or white vinegar
1   teaspoon Dijon-style mustard
⅛   teaspoon ground black pepper
1   bunch watercress or arugula, torn into
    bite-size pieces

Preheat oven to 450°.

In 13 x 9-inch baking or roasting pan, blend Savory
Herb with Garlic Soup Mix and ⅓ cup oil. Add

potatoes; toss until evenly coated. Bake uncovered,
stirring occasionally, 40 minutes or until potatoes
are tender and golden brown.

In large bowl, combine remaining 2 tablespoons oil,
vinegar, mustard and pepper. Add potatoes and
watercress; toss until evenly coated. Makes about
4 servings.

•Also terrific with Lipton Recipe Secrets Golden Herb
with Lemon Soup Mix.

*Watercress is a member of the mustard family and has
a slightly bitter, peppery flavor.*

ROASTED POTATO & WATERCRESS SALAD

CONFETTI RICE PILAF

Prep Time: 5 minutes

Cook Time: 25 minutes

1 tablespoon margarine or butter
1 cup regular or converted rice
1 cup fresh or drained canned sliced mushrooms
2 medium carrots, diced
1 envelope Lipton Recipe Secrets Savory Herb with Garlic Soup Mix
2¼ cups water

In 12-inch skillet, melt margarine over medium-high heat and cook rice, stirring frequently, until golden.

Stir in mushrooms, carrots and Savory Herb with Garlic Soup Mix blended with water. Bring to a boil over high heat. Reduce heat to low and simmer covered 20 minutes or until rice is tender. Makes about 6 servings.

•Also terrific with Lipton Recipe Secrets Golden Herb with Lemon, Golden Onion, Onion-Mushroom or Onion Soup Mix.

Converted rice is a long-grain rice that has been partially steamed before milling, which helps retain nutrients.

SOUTH-OF-THE-BORDER RICE

Prep Time: 5 minutes

Cook Time: 25 minutes

1 tablespoon margarine or butter
4 green onions, diagonally sliced (about ¾ cup)
1 cup regular or converted rice
1 envelope Lipton Recipe Secrets Fiesta Herb with Red Pepper Soup Mix
2½ cups water
½ cup sour cream
1½ cups shredded Monterey Jack or cheddar cheese (about 6 oz.)

In 3-quart saucepan, melt margarine over medium heat and cook green onions, stirring occasionally,

3 minutes. Add rice, stirring to coat. Add Fiesta Herb with Red Pepper Soup Mix blended with water. Bring to a boil over high heat. Reduce heat to low and simmer covered 20 minutes or until rice is tender. Stir in sour cream and cheese; heat through. Makes about 4 servings.

•Also terrific with Lipton Recipe Secrets Savory Herb with Garlic or Golden Onion Soup Mix.

Save time by purchasing pre-shredded cheese in reclosable bags from the refrigerated section of your supermarket.

CONFETTI RICE PILAF

BARLEY CORN SALAD

Prep Time: 15 minutes

Cook Time: 12 minutes
Stand Time: 25 minutes

3   **tablespoons olive or vegetable oil**
1   **cup quick-cooking barley**
1   **envelope Lipton Recipe Secrets Onion Soup Mix**
2   **cups water**
2   **carrots, diced**
1   **small cucumber, peeled, seeded and diced**
1   **cup frozen whole kernel corn, thawed**
3   **tablespoons fresh lemon juice***
¾   **teaspoon dried oregano leaves, crushed**
3   **cups shredded fresh spinach leaves (about 4½ oz.)**
4   **ounces feta or blue cheese, crumbled (optional)**

In 3-quart saucepan, heat 1 tablespoon oil over medium-high heat and cook barley, stirring occasionally, 1 minute or until golden brown. Stir in Onion Soup Mix blended with water. Bring to a boil over high heat. Reduce heat to low and simmer covered 10 minutes or until barley is tender. Remove from heat and let stand covered 5 minutes. Turn barley into large bowl and let stand, stirring occasionally, until cool. Stir in carrots, cucumber and corn.

In small bowl, blend lemon juice, oregano and remaining 2 tablespoons oil; stir into barley mixture. To serve, arrange spinach on serving platter; top with barley salad, then sprinkle with cheese. Makes about 4 main-dish or 8 side-dish servings.

•Also terrific with Lipton Recipe Secrets Savory Herb with Garlic, Golden Herb with Lemon or Golden Onion Soup Mix.

*If using Lipton Recipe Secrets Golden Herb with Lemon Soup Mix, substitute white wine vinegar for lemon juice.

One large lemon will yield about 3 to 4 tablespoons fresh lemon juice.

BARLEY CORN SALAD

THREE-PEPPER RISOTTO

Prep Time: 5 minutes   *Cook Time: 35 minutes*

2 **tablespoons olive or vegetable oil**
3 **medium red, green and/or yellow bell peppers,
    diced**
1½ **cups Arborio, regular or converted rice**
½ **cup dry white wine, vermouth or water**
1 **envelope Lipton Recipe Secrets Savory Herb
    with Garlic Soup Mix**
3½ **cups boiling water**
½ **cup grated Parmesan cheese**

In heavy-duty 3-quart saucepan, heat oil over
medium-high heat and cook red peppers, stirring
occasionally, 5 minutes. Add rice and cook, stirring
constantly, 3 minutes. Slowly add wine and cook,

stirring constantly, until liquid is absorbed. Stir in
Savory Herb with Garlic Soup Mix blended with
1 cup boiling water. Reduce heat to low and simmer
uncovered, stirring frequently, until liquid is
absorbed. Continue adding remaining 2½ cups
boiling water, 1 cup at a time, stirring frequently,
until rice is slightly creamy and just tender. Stir in
cheese. Makes about 4 main-dish or 8 side-dish
servings.

•Also terrific with Lipton Recipe Secrets Golden Herb
with Lemon, Fiesta Herb with Red Pepper, Onion,
Golden Onion or Onion-Mushroom Soup Mix.

*Arborio rice is found in specialty food stores. This high-starch,
shorter, fatter grain rice is used in risotto for its creamy texture.*

DINER SKILLET POTATOES

Prep Time: 15 minutes   *Cook Time: 22 minutes*

1½ **pounds all-purpose potatoes, peeled and diced**
2 **large red and/or green bell peppers, chopped**
1 **envelope Lipton Recipe Secrets Onion Soup Mix**
2 **tablespoons olive or vegetable oil**

In large bowl, combine potatoes, red peppers and
Onion Soup Mix until evenly coated.

In 12-inch nonstick skillet, heat oil over medium
heat and cook potato mixture covered, stirring

occasionally, 12 minutes. Remove cover and continue
cooking, stirring occasionally, 10 minutes or until
potatoes are tender. Makes about 6 servings.

•Also terrific with Lipton Recipe Secrets Fiesta Herb
with Red Pepper Soup Mix.

*Diced refers to chopping ingredients into ¼- to ½-inch
uniform square pieces.*

TWICE-BAKED GARLIC POTATOES

Prep Time: 20 minutes

*Cook Time: 35 minutes if microwaving potatoes
OR 1 hour 15 minutes if oven-baking potatoes*

4   medium baking potatoes (about 8 oz. ea.),
     unpeeled and baked
½   cup milk, heated to boiling
1   envelope Lipton Recipe Secrets Savory Herb
     with Garlic Soup Mix
¼   cup margarine or butter, melted
4   tablespoons grated Parmesan cheese

Preheat oven to 375°.

Cut a lengthwise slice from top of each potato.
Remove skin from the top slice and place pulp in
medium bowl. Scoop pulp from each potato, leaving

¼-inch-thick shells. Add to bowl; add hot milk,
Savory Herb with Garlic Soup Mix, margarine and
3 tablespoons cheese. Mash potatoes. Equally spoon
potato filling into potato shells. Arrange on baking
sheet and sprinkle with remaining 1 tablespoon
cheese. Bake uncovered 15 minutes or until lightly
browned. Makes about 4 servings.

•Also terrific with Lipton Recipe Secrets Golden Herb
with Lemon, Fiesta Herb with Red Pepper or Golden
Onion Soup Mix.

*Bake potatoes about 1 hour at 400°, or pierce potatoes and
microwave at HIGH (Full Power) 20 minutes, turning once.*

ONION-ROASTED POTATOES

Prep Time: 5 minutes

Cook Time: 40 minutes

1   envelope Lipton Recipe Secrets Onion Soup Mix
2   pounds all-purpose potatoes, cut into large chunks
⅓   cup olive or vegetable oil

Preheat oven to 450°.

In large plastic bag or bowl, add all ingredients.
Close bag and shake, or toss in bowl, until potatoes
are evenly coated. In 13 x 9-inch baking or roasting

pan, arrange potatoes; discard bag. Bake uncovered,
stirring occasionally, 40 minutes or until potatoes are
tender and golden brown. Garnish, if desired, with
chopped fresh parsley. Makes about 4 servings.

•Also terrific with Lipton Recipe Secrets Onion-
Mushroom, Savory Herb with Garlic or Fiesta Herb
with Red Pepper Soup Mix.

This recipe is also delicious using red potatoes.

GARLIC FRIES

Prep Time: 10 minutes   *Cook Time: 40 minutes*

1   envelope Lipton Recipe Secrets Savory Herb
      with Garlic Soup Mix
⅓ cup margarine or butter, melted
1   cup plain dry bread crumbs
2   pounds large red potatoes, cut lengthwise
      into wedges

Preheat oven to 400°.

In large bowl, blend Savory Herb with Garlic Soup
Mix with margarine. Place bread crumbs in small
bowl. Add potatoes to soup mixture and toss until
evenly coated. Place potatoes in bread crumbs and
toss until evenly coated. In 15½ x 10½ x 1-inch jelly-
roll pan sprayed with nonstick cooking spray, arrange
potatoes in single layer. Bake uncovered 40 minutes
or until potatoes are tender and golden brown.
Makes about 4 servings.

•Also terrific with Lipton Recipe Secrets Fiesta Herb
with Red Pepper, Onion, Golden Herb with Lemon
or Italian Herb with Tomato Soup Mix.

2 pounds of red potatoes equals about 8 large potatoes.

QUICK VEGETABLE MEDLEY

Prep Time: 5 minutes   *Cook Time: 20 minutes*

2   tablespoons margarine or butter
4   medium carrots, diagonally sliced
4   ribs celery, cut into 1-inch pieces
1   large onion, cut into wedges
1   envelope Lipton Recipe Secrets Golden Herb
      with Lemon Soup Mix
1   cup water
1   tablespoon white vinegar or white wine vinegar

In 10-inch skillet, melt margarine over medium heat
and cook carrots, celery and onion, stirring
occasionally, 5 minutes or until crisp-tender. Add
Golden Herb with Lemon Soup Mix blended with
water and vinegar. Cook covered, stirring
occasionally, 10 minutes or until vegetables are
tender. Makes about 4 servings.

TIP: For a quick main dish, stir leftover cut-up
cooked chicken into vegetables during last 2 minutes
of cooking.

•Also terrific with Lipton Recipe Secrets Savory Herb
with Garlic or Fiesta Herb with Red Pepper Soup Mix.

*To cut an onion into wedges, first cut in half from top to
bottom. Place cut side down and cut lengthwise into wedges.*

GARLIC FRIES

BROCCOLI & RED PEPPER SAUTÉ

Prep Time: 10 minutes   *Cook Time: 12 minutes*

2   tablespoons olive or vegetable oil
4   cups small broccoli florets
1   large red bell pepper, cut into thin strips
1   medium onion, sliced
1   clove garlic, finely chopped
1   envelope Lipton Recipe Secrets Golden Herb
       with Lemon Soup Mix
1   cup water
¼   cup sliced almonds, toasted (optional)

In 12-inch skillet, heat oil over medium heat and cook broccoli, red pepper, onion and garlic, stirring occasionally, 5 minutes or until onion is tender. Add Golden Herb with Lemon Soup Mix blended with water. Simmer covered 5 minutes or until broccoli is tender. Sprinkle with almonds. Makes about 6 servings.

•Also terrific with Lipton Recipe Secrets Savory Herb with Garlic Soup Mix.

2 pounds of broccoli will yield about 4 cups of broccoli florets.

SAVORY GLAZED GREEN BEANS

Prep Time: 5 minutes   *Cook Time: 5 minutes*

1   envelope Lipton Recipe Secrets Savory Herb
       with Garlic Soup Mix
1   cup water
2   tablespoons firmly packed brown sugar
¼   teaspoon salt
1   package (20 oz.) frozen cut green beans, thawed
1   cup frozen pearl onions (about 5 oz.), thawed*

In 2-quart saucepan, bring Savory Herb with Garlic Soup Mix blended with water, sugar and salt to a boil over high heat. Stir in vegetables. Reduce heat to medium and cook uncovered, stirring occasionally, 5 minutes or until vegetables are tender. Makes about 4 servings.

•Also terrific with Lipton Recipe Secrets Golden Herb with Lemon or Golden Onion Soup Mix.

*If using Lipton Recipe Secrets Golden Onion Soup Mix, omit pearl onions.

In a time crunch? Thaw frozen vegetables in the microwave at HIGH (Full Power) about 5 minutes, stirring once.

BROCCOLI & RED PEPPER SAUTÉ

LIPTON CALIFORNIA MASHED POTATOES

Prep Time: 10 minutes   *Cook Time: 25 minutes*

2 **pounds all-purpose potatoes, peeled, if desired, and cut into chunks**
   Water
2 **tablespoons chopped fresh parsley (optional)**
1 **envelope Lipton Recipe Secrets Onion Soup Mix**
¾ **cup milk, heated to boiling**
½ **cup sour cream**

In 3-quart saucepan, cover potatoes with water. Bring to a boil over high heat. Reduce heat to low and simmer uncovered 20 minutes or until potatoes are very tender; drain. Return potatoes to saucepan. Mash potatoes; stir in parsley and Onion Soup Mix blended with hot milk and sour cream. Makes about 6 servings.

•Also terrific with Lipton Recipe Secrets Golden Onion, Golden Herb with Lemon or Savory Herb with Garlic Soup Mix.

2 pounds of all-purpose potatoes equals about 4 medium Idaho potatoes.

SQUASH BAKE

Prep Time: 10 minutes   *Cook Time: 35 minutes*

4 **medium zucchini and/or yellow squash (about 1½ lbs.), diagonally sliced into ¼-inch-thick pieces**
1 **envelope Lipton Recipe Secrets Onion Soup Mix**
2 **tablespoons all-purpose flour**
¼ **teaspoon dried thyme leaves, crushed (optional)**
1 **container (8 oz.) sour cream**
½ **cup milk**
3 **slices bread, cut into ½-inch cubes**
3 **tablespoons margarine or butter, melted**

Preheat oven to 350°.

In 9-inch square baking dish sprayed with nonstick cooking spray, arrange zucchini. In small bowl, with wire whisk, thoroughly blend Onion Soup Mix, flour, thyme and sour cream. Blend in milk until very smooth; pour over zucchini. In bowl, toss bread cubes with margarine until evenly coated; sprinkle over zucchini. Bake uncovered 35 minutes or until zucchini is tender. Makes about 6 servings.

•Also terrific with Lipton Recipe Secrets Golden Onion or Golden Herb with Lemon Soup Mix.

For a shortcut, substitute ½ cup croutons for bread cubes.

OVEN-ROASTED VEGETABLES

Prep Time: 10 minutes　　　　　　　　　　　　　*Cook Time: 20 minutes*

1　envelope Lipton Recipe Secrets Savory Herb
　　with Garlic Soup Mix
1½　pounds assorted fresh vegetables*
2　tablespoons olive or vegetable oil

Preheat oven to 450°. In large plastic bag or bowl,
add all ingredients. Close bag and shake, or toss in
bowl, until vegetables are evenly coated. In 13 x 9-
inch baking or roasting pan, arrange vegetables;
discard bag. Bake uncovered, stirring once,
20 minutes or until vegetables are tender.
Makes about 4 servings.

*Use any combination of the following, sliced:
zucchini, yellow squash, red, green or yellow bell
peppers, carrots, celery and mushrooms.

•Also terrific with Lipton Recipe Secrets Golden Herb
with Lemon, Italian Herb with Tomato, Onion or
Golden Onion Soup Mix.

*Vegetables may also be grilled on a grill screen or in foil
packets. Grill screens are available in the housewares section
of department stores or hardware stores.*

HOME-STYLE CORN CAKES

Prep Time: 10 minutes　　　　　　　　　　　　　*Cook Time: 15 minutes*

1　cup yellow cornmeal
½　cup all-purpose flour
½　teaspoon baking powder
½　teaspoon baking soda
1　envelope Lipton Recipe Secrets Onion Soup Mix
¾　cup buttermilk
1　egg, beaten
1　can (17¼ oz.) cream-style corn
2　ounces roasted red peppers, chopped (about ¼ cup)
　　Butter

In large bowl, combine cornmeal, flour, baking
powder and baking soda. Stir in Onion Soup Mix

blended with buttermilk, egg, corn and roasted red
peppers. In 12-inch nonstick skillet or on griddle,
melt ½ teaspoon butter over medium heat. Drop ¼
cup batter for each corn cake and cook, turning once,
5 minutes or until cooked through and golden brown.
Remove to serving platter and keep warm. Repeat
with remaining batter and additional butter if
needed. Serve, if desired, with sour cream and
prepared salsa. Makes about 18 corn cakes.

•Also terrific with Lipton Recipe Secrets Golden
Onion or Fiesta Herb with Red Pepper Soup Mix.

*Leftover corn cakes may be frozen. Reheat straight from
the freezer in preheated 350° oven for 15 minutes.*

CASUAL ENTERTAINING

ITALIAN STUFFED PINWHEELS

Prep Time: 10 minutes   *Cook Time: 12 minutes*

1 **envelope Lipton Recipe Secrets Italian Herb
      with Tomato Soup Mix**
2 **packages (3 oz. ea.) cream cheese, softened**
1 **cup shredded mozzarella cheese (about 4 oz.)**
1 **tablespoon grated Parmesan cheese**
2 **tablespoons milk**
1 **package (10 oz.) refrigerated pizza crust**

Preheat oven to 375°.

In large bowl, blend Italian Herb with Tomato Soup
Mix, cream cheese, mozzarella cheese, Parmesan
cheese and milk; set aside.

Unroll pizza crust, then evenly top with filling. Roll,
starting with long side, jelly-roll style. Cut into ¾-inch
rounds*. On baking sheet sprayed with nonstick
cooking spray, arrange rounds, cut side down. Bake
uncovered 12 minutes or until golden. Makes about
16 pinwheels.

*If rolled pizza crust is too soft to cut, chill or freeze
until firm.

•Also terrific with Lipton Recipe Secrets Savory Herb
with Garlic Soup Mix.

Pinwheels make a great party appetizer or after-school snack.

ITALIAN STUFFED PINWHEELS

WHITE PIZZA DIP

1   **envelope Lipton Recipe Secrets Savory Herb with Garlic Soup Mix**
1   **container (8 oz.) sour cream**
1   **cup (8 oz.) ricotta cheese**
1   **cup shredded mozzarella cheese (about 4 oz.)**
¼   **cup (1 oz.) chopped pepperoni (optional)**
1   **loaf Italian or French bread, sliced**

Preheat oven to 350°. In shallow 1-quart casserole, combine Savory Herb with Garlic Soup Mix, sour cream, ricotta cheese, ¾ cup mozzarella cheese and pepperoni. Sprinkle with remaining ¼ cup mozzarella

cheese. Bake uncovered 30 minutes or until heated through. Serve with bread. Makes about 2 cups dip.

Variations:

TRADITIONAL-STYLE PIZZA DIP: Substitute 1 envelope Lipton Recipe Secrets Italian Herb with Tomato Soup Mix for Savory Herb with Garlic Soup Mix.

SPICY-STYLE PIZZA DIP: Substitute 1 envelope Lipton Recipe Secrets Fiesta Herb with Red Pepper Soup Mix for Savory Herb with Garlic Soup Mix.

Try THE FAMOUS LIPTON CALIFORNIA DIP! In small bowl, thoroughly combine 1 envelope Onion Soup Mix with 16 ounces sour cream. Chill at least 2 hours. (This recipe is also delicious with all Lipton Recipe Secrets varieties.)

CAN'T GET ENOUGH CHICKEN WINGS

12   **chicken wings (about 2 lbs.)**
½   **cup margarine or butter, melted**
1   **envelope Lipton Recipe Secrets Savory Herb with Garlic Soup Mix**
1   **teaspoon cayenne pepper sauce (optional)***

Cut tips off chicken wings (save tips for soup). Cut chicken wings in half at joint. Deep fry, bake or broil

until golden brown and crunchy. In medium bowl, blend margarine, Savory Herb with Garlic Soup Mix and pepper sauce. Add hot cooked chicken wings; toss until evenly coated. Serve, if desired, over greens with cut-up celery. Makes 24 appetizers.

*Use more or less according to taste desired.

Freeze wing tips in a freezer storage bag. Add to stock pot when making soup for extra chicken flavor.

CARROT-GINGER SOUP

Prep Time: 15 minutes

Cook Time: 35 minutes

2 tablespoons margarine or butter
1 pound carrots, chopped
1 medium all-purpose potato (about 8 oz.),
    peeled and diced
1 (1-in.) piece fresh ginger, peeled and sliced, or
    ½ teaspoon ground ginger
1 envelope Lipton Recipe Secrets Onion Soup Mix
4 cups water
½ cup whipping or heavy cream or light cream

In 3-quart saucepan, melt margarine over medium heat and cook carrots, potato and ginger, covered, stirring occasionally, 10 minutes. Stir in Onion Soup Mix blended with water. Bring to a boil over high heat. Reduce heat to low and simmer uncovered, stirring occasionally, 20 minutes or until vegetables are tender. In blender, puree soup in batches until smooth. Return pureed soup to saucepan and stir in cream; heat through. Sprinkle, if desired, with chopped chives or green onions. Makes about 5 cups soup.

•Also terrific with Lipton Recipe Secrets Golden Onion or Golden Herb with Lemon Soup Mix.

Make soup ahead and then freeze while still warm, leaving a little room at the top of the containers for expanding.

SOUTHWESTERN VEGETABLE DIP

Prep Time: 10 minutes

Chill Time: 2 hours

1 envelope Lipton Recipe Secrets Fiesta Herb
    with Red Pepper Soup Mix
1 container (16 oz.) sour cream
1 small tomato, finely chopped
½ cup finely chopped green bell pepper
¼ cup finely chopped onion

In medium bowl, thoroughly combine all ingredients; cover and chill at least 2 hours. Serve, if desired, with cut-up fresh vegetables, bread sticks or tortilla chips. Makes about 2½ cups dip.

TIP: Serve dip in hollowed-out red, green or yellow bell peppers.

•Also terrific with Lipton Recipe Secrets Savory Herb with Garlic Soup Mix.

Any cold dip made with sour cream may be safely stored in the refrigerator up to 3 days.

GARLIC STEAMED MUSSELS

Prep Time: 20 minutes   **Cook Time: 10 minutes**

- ¾ **cup dry white wine or water**
- ½ **cup water**
- 3 **dozen mussels, well scrubbed and beards removed**
- 1 **envelope Lipton Recipe Secrets Savory Herb with Garlic Soup Mix**
  Crusty French or Italian bread

In Dutch oven or 6-quart saucepot, bring wine and water to a boil over high heat. Add mussels; return to a boil. Reduce heat to low and simmer covered 3 minutes or until mussels open. With slotted spoon, remove mussels to large bowl; discard any unopened shells. Strain liquid from Dutch oven using strainer lined with cheesecloth or paper towels. Reserve enough liquid to equal 1½ cups; rinse and wipe pot clean. In same Dutch oven, bring Savory Herb with Garlic Soup Mix blended with reserved 1½ cups liquid to a boil over high heat. Pour over mussels. Serve with bread. Makes about 6 servings.

•Also terrific with Lipton Recipe Secrets Golden Herb with Lemon Soup Mix.

Purchase mussels with tightly closed shells or those that quickly close when tapped. Avoid those that sound hollow.

SEAFOOD IN PINK SAUCE

Prep Time: 20 minutes   **Cook Time: 15 minutes**

- 3 **tablespoons margarine or butter**
- 1 **large bunch green onions, sliced**
- 4 **ounces mushrooms, sliced**
- ¼ **cup sherry, dry white wine or water**
- 1 **envelope Lipton Recipe Secrets Italian Herb with Tomato Soup Mix**
- 1¼ **cups milk**
- ½ **pound uncooked medium shrimp, peeled and deveined**
- ½ **pound bay scallops**
  Hot cooked orzo pasta, linguine or rice

In 12-inch skillet, melt margarine over medium heat and cook green onions and mushrooms, stirring frequently, 10 minutes or until very tender. Add sherry and cook 1 minute. Add Italian Herb with Tomato Soup Mix blended with milk. Bring to the boiling point over high heat. Stir in shrimp and scallops. Reduce heat to medium and cook 3 minutes or until shrimp turn pink and scallops are opaque. Serve over hot pasta. Makes about 4 servings.

•Also terrific with Lipton Recipe Secrets Fiesta Herb with Red Pepper, Golden Herb with Lemon or Savory Herb with Garlic Soup Mix.

For an extra time-saver, purchase shrimp that have already been peeled and deveined.

GARLIC STEAMED MUSSELS

PORK CHOPS BURGUNDY

Prep Time: 5 minutes   *Cook Time: 1 hour 10 minutes*

2 tablespoons olive or vegetable oil
4 bone-in or boneless pork chops, 1 inch thick
1 package (8 or 10 oz.) mushrooms, halved
1 clove garlic, finely chopped
1 envelope Lipton Recipe Secrets Onion-Mushroom
   Soup Mix
1 can (8 oz.) tomato sauce
½ cup dry red wine or water
   Hot cooked rice

Preheat oven to 350°.

In 12-inch skillet, heat oil over medium-high heat and brown chops. Remove chops to 13 x 9-inch baking or roasting pan and set aside; reserve drippings. Add mushrooms and garlic to reserved drippings and cook over medium heat, stirring occasionally, 1 minute. Stir in Onion-Mushroom Soup

Mix blended with tomato sauce and wine. Bring to a boil over high heat; pour over chops. Bake uncovered 1 hour or until chops are done. Serve with hot rice. Makes about 4 servings.

Variations:

VEAL CHOPS BURGUNDY: Substitute 4 veal loin or rib chops for pork. Prepare as above, decreasing bake time to 30 minutes.

LAMB CHOPS BURGUNDY: Substitute 8 lamb loin or rib chops for pork. Prepare as above, decreasing bake time to 20 minutes.

•Also terrific with Lipton Recipe Secrets Onion or Savory Herb with Garlic Soup Mix.

A good rule of thumb when cooking with wine–only use the quality of wine you would also drink.

PENNE ALLA VODKA

Prep Time: 10 minutes   *Cook Time: 10 minutes*

2 tablespoons margarine or butter
1 medium onion, chopped
1 clove garlic, finely chopped*
1 envelope Lipton Recipe Secrets Italian Herb
     with Tomato Soup Mix
1½ cups milk
2 tablespoons vodka, sherry or water
⅛ teaspoon crushed red pepper flakes (optional)
1 cup frozen green peas, thawed
8 ounces penne or ziti pasta, cooked and drained

In 12-inch skillet, melt margarine over medium heat
and cook onion and garlic, stirring occasionally,

5 minutes or until onion is tender. Stir in Italian Herb
with Tomato Soup Mix blended with milk, vodka and
pepper. Bring to the boiling point over high heat. Stir
in peas. Reduce heat to low and simmer uncovered
2 minutes. Toss with hot pasta. Serve immediately.
Makes about 2 main-dish or 4 side-dish servings.

•Also terrific with Lipton Recipe Secrets Fiesta Herb
with Red Pepper, Golden Herb with Lemon or Savory
Herb with Garlic Soup Mix.

*If using Lipton Recipe Secrets Savory Herb with
Garlic Soup Mix, omit garlic.

Penne is tubular pasta, smooth or ridged, that is cut
diagonally on both ends. Ziti is wider tubed pasta,
smooth or ridged.

OVEN-BAKED BOURGUIGNONNE

Prep Time: 15 minutes

Cook Time: 2 hours

2 pounds boneless beef chuck or round steak,
   cut into 1-inch cubes
¼ cup all-purpose flour
1⅓ cups sliced carrots
1 can (14½ oz.) whole peeled tomatoes, undrained
   and chopped
1 bay leaf
1 envelope Lipton Recipe Secrets Onion Soup Mix
½ cup dry red wine or water
1 cup fresh or canned sliced mushrooms
1 package (8 oz.) medium or broad egg noodles,
   cooked and drained

Preheat oven to 400°.

In 2-quart casserole, toss beef with flour, then bake uncovered 20 minutes. Add carrots, tomatoes and bay leaf, then Onion Soup Mix blended with wine. Bake covered 1½ hours or until beef is tender. Stir in mushrooms and bake covered an additional 10 minutes. Remove bay leaf. Serve over hot noodles. Makes about 8 servings.

•Also terrific with Lipton Recipe Secrets Beefy Onion, Onion-Mushroom or Beefy Mushroom Soup Mix.

Bourguignonne is a French word that means "as prepared in Burgundy, France."

OVEN-BAKED BOURGUIGNONNE

DELECTABLE BEEF STROGANOFF

Prep Time: 10 minutes   *Cook Time: 55 minutes*

2 tablespoons margarine or butter
2 pounds boneless beef round or chuck steak,
    cut into thin strips
8 ounces mushrooms, sliced
1 envelope Lipton Recipe Secrets Onion Soup Mix
2¼ cups water
2 tablespoons all-purpose flour
½ cup sour cream
    Hot cooked noodles

In 12-inch skillet, melt margarine over medium-high heat and brown beef with mushrooms. Add Onion Soup Mix blended with 1¾ cups water. Bring to a boil over high heat. Reduce heat to low; simmer covered, stirring, 40 minutes or until beef is tender. Stir in flour blended with sour cream and remaining ½ cup water. Bring to the boiling point over high heat. Reduce heat to low and simmer, stirring contstantly, until sauce is thickened, about 5 minutes. Serve over hot noodles. Makes about 8 servings.

•Also terrific with Lipton Recipe Secrets Onion-Mushroom, Beefy Mushroom or Beefy Onion Soup Mix.

For easier slicing, partially freeze beef until firm.

ROAST LOIN OF PORK WITH GARLIC

Prep Time: 5 minutes *Cook Time: 1 hour*

1 envelope Lipton Recipe Secrets Onion Soup Mix
2 tablespoons olive or vegetable oil
1 clove garlic, finely chopped*
1 tablespoon water
1 slice bacon, crisp-cooked and crumbled
1 3½-pound boneless pork loin roast

Preheat oven to 350°. In small bowl, combine all ingredients except pork. In 13 x 9-inch baking or roasting pan, arrange pork. With knife, score (lightly cut) top of pork. Spoon soup mixture evenly over pork. Bake uncovered 1 hour or until meat thermometer reaches 160°. Makes about 8 servings.

•Also terrific with Lipton Recipe Secrets Golden Herb with Lemon, Savory Herb with Garlic, Fiesta Herb with Red Pepper or Onion-Mushroom Soup Mix.

*If using Lipton Recipe Secrets Savory Herb with Garlic Soup Mix, omit garlic.

Why score meat? It helps the meat absorb more flavor and is also used as a decoration.

GARLIC 'N LEMON ROAST CHICKEN

Prep Time: 10 minutes

Marinate Time: 2 hours
Cook Time: 1 hour 20 minutes

1 **small onion, finely chopped**
1 **envelope Lipton Recipe Secrets Savory Herb**
   with Garlic Soup Mix
2 **tablespoons olive or vegetable oil**
2 **tablespoons lemon juice***
1 **3½-pound roasting chicken**

In large plastic bag or bowl, combine onion and Savory Herb with Garlic Soup Mix blended with oil and lemon juice; add chicken. Close bag and shake, or toss in bowl, until chicken is evenly coated. Cover and marinate in refrigerator, turning occasionally, 2 hours.

Preheat oven to 350°. Remove chicken and marinade to 13 x 9-inch baking or roasting pan. Arrange chicken, breast side up; discard bag. Bake uncovered, basting occasionally, 1 hour 20 minutes or until meat thermometer reaches 180°. Makes about 4 servings.

NOTE: Insert meat thermometer into thickest part of thigh between breast and thigh; make sure tip does not touch bone.

•Also terrific with Lipton Recipe Secrets Golden Herb with Lemon, Fiesta Herb with Red Pepper or Italian Herb with Tomato Soup Mix.

*If using Lipton Recipe Secrets Golden Herb with Lemon Soup Mix, omit lemon juice.

Serve with Lipton Rice & Sauce—Chicken Flavor or Rice Medley for a complementary side dish.

GRILLED TUNA SALAD

Prep Time: 15 minutes

Marinate Time: 30 minutes–1 hour
Cook Time: 15 minutes

1   **envelope Lipton Recipe Secrets Golden Herb**
      with Lemon Soup Mix
½   **cup dry white wine or water**
¾   **cup water**
1   **pound tuna, swordfish or salmon steaks**
8   **cups assorted mixed greens***
3   **tablespoons sour cream**
⅓   **cup chopped pecans, toasted, if desired (optional)**

In large, shallow nonaluminum baking dish or plastic bag, blend Golden Herb with Lemon Soup Mix, wine and water. Add fish; turn to coat. Cover, or close bag, and marinate in refrigerator, turning once, up to 1 hour.

Meanwhile, arrange greens on serving platter. Remove fish from marinade, reserving marinade. Grill, broil or pan-fry fish, turning once, until done. In small saucepan, bring reserved marinade to a boil over high heat and continue boiling 2 minutes. Remove from heat and with wire whisk, blend in sour cream. Cut fish into chunks and arrange over greens. Drizzle with warm marinade mixture and sprinkle with pecans. Makes about 4 main-dish servings.

*Use any of the following: radicchio, endive, watercress, arugula or leaf lettuce.

•Also terrific with Lipton Recipe Secrets Savory Herb with Garlic Soup Mix.

Grill fish for about 10 minutes per inch thickness, turning once.

GARLIC-CRUMB-COATED SWORDFISH

Prep Time: 10 minutes

Cook Time: 25 minutes

1   **envelope Lipton Recipe Secrets Savory Herb**
      with Garlic Soup Mix
1   **cup fresh bread crumbs**
1   **medium plum tomato, chopped**
2   **tablespoons margarine or butter, melted**
6   **swordfish, tuna or salmon steaks**

Preheat oven to 375°. In bowl, combine Savory Herb with Garlic Soup Mix, bread crumbs, tomato and

margarine. In 13 x 9-inch baking or roasting pan, arrange fish. Evenly top fish with crumb mixture, patting lightly. Bake uncovered 25 minutes or until fish flakes. Makes about 6 servings.

•Also terrific with Lipton Recipe Secrets Golden Herb with Lemon or Golden Onion Soup Mix.

When purchasing fresh fish steaks, look for flesh with a clean appearance, firm, moist texture and no fishy odor.

GRILLED TUNA SALAD

BOUILLABAISSE

Prep Time: 20 minutes

Cook Time: 15 minutes

12 thin slices French bread
1 clove garlic
1 tablespoon olive or vegetable oil
2 medium carrots, sliced
1 medium bulb fennel, trimmed, halved, cored
    and sliced or 2 ribs celery, sliced
1 small onion, chopped
¼ cup dry white wine or water
1 envelope Lipton Recipe Secrets Fiesta Herb
    with Red Pepper Soup Mix
2 cups water
1 dozen little neck clams, well scrubbed
1 pound uncooked large shrimp, peeled and deveined
½ pound firm white fish fillets (such as cod
    or halibut), cut into 1-inch pieces

On broiler pan, arrange bread slices. Broil bread, turning once, 1½ minutes or until golden brown. Rub one side of each bread slice with garlic; set aside.

In Dutch oven or 6-quart saucepot, heat oil over medium heat and cook carrots, fennel and onion, stirring occasionally, 5 minutes. Stir in wine. Bring to a boil over high heat and continue boiling 1 minute. Stir in Fiesta Herb with Red Pepper Soup Mix blended with water; return to a boil. Add clams; reduce heat to medium and cook covered 3 minutes or until clams begin to open. Add shrimp and fish; continue cooking covered 1 minute or until shrimp turn pink and fish flakes. (Discard any unopened clam shells.) Serve with garlic toast. Makes about 4 servings.

•Also terrific with Lipton Recipe Secrets Italian Herb with Tomato, Savory Herb with Garlic or Golden Herb with Lemon Soup Mix.

Bouillabaisse is a seafood stew that originated in Provence, France. It is traditionally served with crusty French bread.